THE PURCHASE OF THIS BOOK INCLUDES CAREER LONG TELE-MENTORING

*"My coach is the nation's leading expert.
That's why I am 184% of quota!"*
David Wilson, Charleston, North Carolina

Anthony Parinello, personal success coach to over one million professionals, will guide you step-by-step on the journey to your own success! This one-of-a-kind commitment is without equal. No other author has devoted more personal time, energy, and passion to the success of others.

*"Tony is FOR REAL! Real experience,
real ideas, and real commitment to his student's
success."*
Vinnie Deschamps, San Jose, California

Each month you'll have an opportunity to join Anthony Parinello's tele-conference calls. Ask the critical question to make the sale, or listen to other people's challenges as they make their way to VITO's office and total success!

*"In the last seven months, my team has generated $18
million in new sales. We couldn't have done it without
Tony's tele-mentoring!"*
Mike Adami, San Ramon, CA

Don't miss one day of tele-mentoring!
Mail your sales receipt for this book along with a SASE to:
Parinello Incorporated
P.O. Box 875
Julian, California 92036
Your mentoring calling card will be sent to you immediately!

"Inspiring and full of unique ideas."
— Heather Brink, San Francisco, California

"Real-world concepts that can be taken with you and used the very next day."
— Ron Gadek, Oak Brook, Illinois

"This is how we need to sell in the remainder of the `90s and beyond."
— Don Stout, West Chester, Pennsylvania

"Tony is a salesperson's sales trainer!"
— Thomas Smith, Chicago, Illinois

"Implementing these ideas may be the only way for salespeople to survive in telecommunications today."
— Dan Liljeberg, Paramus, New Jersey

"Absolutely mandatory for my company—but not for my competitors."
— Joe Emmert, Washington, D.C.

"The best single sales course I've seen in the last fifteen years."
— Ed O'Reilly, Camden, New Jersey

"Will take you to the next income level if you invest the time and energy. Fantastic!"
— Tim Gargain, Memphis, Tennessee

"Differentiates you from every other salesman who calls."
— Mark Reese, St. Louis, Missouri

SELLING TOVITO

SELLING
toVITO

THE VERY IMPORTANT TOP OFFICER

ANTHONY PARINELLO

ADAMS MEDIA CORPORATION
Holbrook, Massachusetts

Published by Adams Media Corporation
260 Center Street, Holbrook, MA 02343

ISBN: 1-55850-386-2

Printed in the United States of America.

S   R   Q   P   O   N   M   L

Library of Congress Cataloging-in-Publication Data
Parinello, Anthony.
Selling to VITO : top-drawer advice for selling to the top floor /
Anthony Parinello.
p.   cm.
Includes index.
ISBN 1-55850-386-2
1. Sales personnel—Training of. 2. Selling—Personnel management.
3. Executives.
I. Title.
HF5439.8.P37   1994
658.85—dc20   94-15481
CIP

This publication is designed to provide accurate and authoritative information
with regard to the subject matter covered. It is sold with the understanding that
the publisher is not engaged in rendering legal, accounting, or other professional
advice. If legal advice or other expert assistance is required, the services of a
competent professional person should be sought.
— From a *Declaration of Principles* jointly adopted by a Committee of the
American Bar Association and a Committee of Publishers and Associations

Cover design: Marshall Henrichs.

This book is available at quantity discounts for bulk purchases.
For information, call 1-800-872-5627 (in Massachusetts, call 781-767-8100).

Visit our home page at hhtp://www.adamsmedia.com

To my beloved mother Josephine Rose Parinello,
for her unshakable love, guidance, support, and confidence
in me—and for teaching me right from wrong.
And to my greatest teacher and mentor my brother Al,
who left this world too soon. I will continually strive to
make them both proud of me.

CONTENTS

FOREWORD

Tony Parinello is amazing.

He is one of the most imaginative and determined people I've ever met. That imagination is apparent the minute you pick up his book or audiotape album and see the name VITO describing the top person in an organization—the Very Important Top Officer with the ultimate "veto" power. Seldom have I known a name or word to take hold so quickly—to become such an integral part of the sales culture. "VITO" is an overnight addition to the lexicon!

Walk into the sales department of any company that has participated in one of Tony's programs and you'll hear managers asking their salespeople, "Have you talked to VITO yet?" You'll hear salespeople saying, "I have a meeting with VITO scheduled for next Tuesday" or "I met VITO—she gave me the go-ahead to do a corporate-wide study!"

Tony's not afraid of challenges or changes. From getting his first job in sales after a tour in the Navy as an airman, to starting his own sales training company, Tony has always stretched beyond his own comfort zone. He sets the bar high, higher than he's ever had it before, and then goes for it.

He's not a perfectionist (that takes too much time), but he always strives for excellence in whatever he does. When he falls short, he picks himself up and tries again. When I asked Tony where he got his determination, he said, "From growing up in the inner city. Hoboken, New Jersey was a rough town. I learned a lot about risks and taking chances, and how to size up challenges on the spot. Watching my dad in the ring—he was a Golden Gloves fighter—was invaluable. I learned that you can't stay down for long if you want to win."

Tony shows that kind of courage and determination in the field he chose to speak and write about. He has taken the most unpopular topic in sales training—prospecting and selling to hard-to-reach top decision makers—and given it new life, spirit, and excitement. Tony challenges and exhilarates even the most experienced salespeople. He doesn't just preach about how important prospecting is, or tell you that it's "all a numbers game." He's developed a comprehensive, logical, and innovative sequence of steps that will *get you to the top decision maker.*

His is a process that is based on twenty-three years of award-winning sales performance—in other words, Tony's own trial and error, with his own feet in the street. In that period of time, Tony made over sixteen thousand prospecting calls to top decision makers and conducted hundreds of interviews with receptionists and executive secretaries all across the nation. He listened to these people carefully. He knows what they want, what they expect, what makes them see red. And he knows how to get their attention. As a behavioral scientist, I can easily see and understand why his unique methods for building trust and rapport with decision makers work so well—and result in appointments.

Tony redefines many of the most outdated beliefs about selling; my favorite example of this has to do with the idea of "closing the sale." Tony never "closes" a sale. He "opens" business relationships, mutually beneficial partnerships that last for many, many years.

Keep in mind that Tony is a tactician—a salesperson's sales trainer. He uses the methods in this book every day; he never suggests an idea that he hasn't already found to be effective in his own sales work. He takes full responsibility for his ideas, a trait that is essential for any professional. Simply stated, he walks his talk.

In my newest audiotape album, "Time to Win," I address the idea that success depends on choice, not chance. Your decisions are what cause your rewards and the consequences you face. Let's think, for example, about the decision of who to call on first in a new prospect company. Clearly, that's a choice you have to make just about every day of your sales career. Tony makes clear that it's also a choice that will have a greater impact on your level of success than virtually any other. In my tape, I also talk about the Statue of Responsibility, a counterpart to the Statue of Liberty that serves as a reminder of lost freedoms and opportunities arising as a result of irresponsible choices and actions. Tony argues persuasively that one of those lost opportunities is neglecting to call at the top. (And he points out that if you don't do it, your competition will!)

Calling at the highest level first is certainly not the easiest, safest, or most comfortable route. But risk—and even a certain amount of discomfort—can be healthy parts of growing, of seeking out opportunities, of learning. And it's been my personal experience that the road less traveled is the one that often pays the biggest dividends in the long run.

When you're talking about getting appointments with VITOs, the dividends will take the form of time saved, opportunity coverage, and customer loyalty—not to mention increased commissions for you, if only because you won't be wasting as much time as before. My guess is that, on some level, you probably already know about the potential advantages of calling too high—and the perils of calling too low—in a prospect organization. So let's move on to the real challenge, making the initial contact with VITO.

That's where Tony's *Selling to VITO* program comes in—and where you will come to benefit from his imagination and his street-smart instincts. His innovative ideas and proven tactics *will* separate you from your competition. Try them and see.

If you were to compare the process of selling to top decision makers to a competitive sports event, you'd have to liken it to a marathon. Like a marathon, half of the job of selling to VITO is preparing yourself, and the other half is employing the proper psychological and tactical edge. If you prepare properly, then use all the advantages at your disposal, you will know, without any doubt, that you can attain your goal. And then you will go out and do just that.

With Tony as your coach and *Selling to VITO* as your training guide, you'll not only finish the marathon—you'll become unstoppable. You'll develop unshakable confidence. You'll set your next goal higher, higher perhaps than you've ever set it before. And you'll make success your own.

— DR. DENIS WAITLEY

ACKNOWLEDGMENTS

My thanks go to the thousands of customers and alumni who continue to put me and my material to the ultimate test every time I conduct a training session. Your challenges and contributions, always solicited and always appreciated, have helped make *Selling to VITO* the program it is.

Grateful acknowledgment, too, is due to the individual family members who are an active part of Parinello, Incorporated: my father, who has always been a sounding board for my ideas and a strong influence in my values and judgment; my wife Nancy, who puts tireless effort into my career; my loyal assistant and best raving fan, Diane Durbin whose long hours, dedication and belief play a major role in my continued success; and my mother-in-law Betty, whose computer expertise and technical advice have been an incredible help.

I want to thank Marya Lintz for lighting a fire under me early on in my sales career.

I'm grateful to all the wonderful people at Adams Media Corporation, including: Brandon Toropov—simply the best—and Dick Staron, who showed the patience of a saint throughout this project's development.

Finally, my thanks go out to you, my new friend and sales associate, for picking this up. You and I have a lot in common.

INTRODUCTION

My favorite introduction is a brief one. Accordingly, I'll keep this short and leave you with one thought before you embark on this program: Check your preconceptions at the door.

This book will show you how to develop more long-term, quality sales than you ever would have imagined possible . . . but to take advantage of it you'll have to change the way you think about "selling." More accurately, you'll have to learn to stop "selling" altogether, and you'll have to learn to take some risks and make some unfamiliar moves. But if you listen to what I have to say, my guess is that you, like thousands of salespeople I've trained all over North America, will agree that the changes I suggest are well worth trying.

And "trying" is the operative word here. Between these covers you will find many approaches you are likely, at first, to consider a little out of the ordinary. They are. Try them anyway. You can always go back to the way you've sold up to this point. (Although I promise you here that if you follow the steps I outline, you will not want to.)

So—keep an open mind. Your career and your success are what's at stake. Even if what I suggest isn't what you're used to doing, isn't what other people in your office are doing, or sounds flat-out crazy, try it anyway. Take my word for it. You'll like what happens.

— ANTHONY PARINELLO

Chapter One:
The Time Is Right

Welcome to the new economy. If you're a salesperson, you have your work cut out for you.

It's more difficult than ever to sell for a living, and every salesperson who's likely to still have a job twelve months from today knows it. The competition is tough, and finding new customers (not to mention keeping the old ones) can be brutal. Prices are down, the cost of sales is up, overhead is up, margins are down. More than ever, companies are looking for strategic alliances and business partnerships today, not quick fixes. And how about the latest trend in the sales world—the moves by companies to tie the commissions of their salespeople to the profitability of the company (or the sale recorded by the rep)? This can mean that if a salesperson spends too much time in an account trying to get an order, then that time and the associated cost of sales is going to be reflected in that salesperson's paycheck. Companies today are also tying customer service responses to the compensation their salespeople receive. And, in yet another twist, there are new payment schemes whereby salespeople are penalized if a company bails out, say, three or four months after signing on. Those "short-term" sales, the ones that relied on low price or a less-than-perfect match with the customer's needs, are being noticed. And, more and more, they're costing salespeople money.

Things just aren't the way they used to be. Today's difficult, surrealistically fast-paced business climate is probably one of the main reasons you bought this book in the first place.

You probably know about all this. And while you may consider this state of affairs to be pretty desperate, I have a surprise for you. It's *because* you know about how difficult things can be these days that you have a remarkable opportunity with today's most important businesspeople. Top decision makers—whom I call VITOs, short for Very Important Top Officers—know all about the often-intense market pressures you face. They deal with those pressures every moment of every working day. VITOs, of course, come in both genders. They are presidents, CEOs, executive vice presidents, and the like. Actually, the titles aren't as important as the function. VITOs have the ultimate veto power in an organization. They have power, control, and authority. They're the people who can say "yes" and have it stick when everyone else is saying "no." They're the people who are most concerned with gaining market share, increasing revenues, controlling expenses, decreasing expenses, reducing time to market, and dealing with the changes in our unpredictable economy. They're the people who have to focus on solutions—and, in that, they have something in common with you.

Perhaps you've tried selling to top decision makers before—and perhaps you found the experience intimidating. Perhaps a VITO gave you the impression that he or she considered all salespeople to be timewasters who are simply never worth bothering with. (Actually, VITOs consider only *bad* salespeople to be timewasters, and they're right.) You may even have come away from your encounter with a VITO convinced that he or she was speaking a completely different language than the one used by most of your contacts. However, most VITOs have sold for a living at one time or another—or, at the very least, appreciate the value of good salespeople.

It's true, VITOs do tend to see the world in terms that are a little different than most of the other people you sell to. While other low-level contacts may worry about protecting their turf, or impressing others in the organization, or even holding on to a position they consider shaky, VITO's interests are usually much more straightforward. VITO wants to *improve the company's bottom line* by raising revenues, lowering expenses, or improving efficiency. Not surprisingly, the language VITO speaks when it comes to dealing with the rest of the business world is a little more direct, a little less patient than that of your average contact. But don't worry. You can reach and do business with VITOs, no matter what your past experiences in dealing with them may have been. If you follow my advice, you'll understand that there's a food chain in every sale. VITO is at the top; the other people in the organization are lower. As a general rule, salespeople make their biggest mistake when they initiate contact at a comparatively low point on the chain!

One of the purposes of this book is to teach you VITO's language—and show you how to use it to your (and VITO's) benefit. The techniques you'll be learning about have worked for tens of thousands of salespeople in businesses throughout the country. They can work for you.

Once you finish reading this book, you will no longer be a distraction for VITO. You will no longer be something that stands in the way of VITO's attempt to deal with today's value-sensitive, ultra-competitive market conditions. You will be *someone*, not something—and an extremely important someone at that. You will be someone who understands what VITO is up against and knows how to offer what VITO wants most to find: *solutions*.

You will be VITO's business partner.

Once you've done that, you won't have to worry about most of the things salespeople keep complaining about. You won't have to worry about getting shunted off to a lower level. You won't have to ask yourself who really has the decision-making authority. You won't be left without any recourse if some specialist within the company decides he doesn't like what you have to offer.

You won't have to worry about any of that because you'll be working, not with just anyone within the organization, but with VITO. And I can tell you working with VITO makes sense because it's what turned my own career around.

Selling to VITO affects the entire sales cycle. Unlike many other sales training programs, where you might approach qualifying, questioning, and closing as separate components, the program you're about to learn is about ideas, tactics, and methods that will move the sales in such a way that you save time, avoid grief, and *compress* the standard sales cycle, so that it runs according to a new and accelerated time frame: VITO's time frame. This makes selling more enjoyable and rewarding, and that's no small feat.

Who Is This Guy?

Let me tell you a little bit about myself. In addition to being an author and a radio host, I'm a salesperson—and I'm also a sales trainer.

As you read this book, you're going to come across a lot of suggestions about ways to do things differently. I know that's sometimes hard to do once you've built up a routine in your sales work. But you should know that I will never, under any circumstances, offer you any advice or outline any technique that is not something I myself have tried and found successful—and continue to use daily.

The ideas in this book are practical, down-to-earth, and, most important of all, proven to work in today's business environment. Try them and see. These are not the theoretical constructs of some business-school whiz. I'm a salesperson, like you, and I think my revenue and commissions over the years indicate that I'm a pretty darned good one.

Right now I'm going to give you a little bit of background to demonstrate that to you. But remember, what I've done isn't the issue here. It's what *you* can do. I'm bringing up my own career because I think talking about it here will make you want to listen to what I have to say on the topic of selling to VITO. And that was what made all the difference for me.

When you get right down to it, though, it would be a little misleading to say that I actually *wanted* to sell to VITO in the early days. The truth was, I was in such a horrible situation that I had no other choice.

I started out as a sales rep for Hewlett-Packard. You had to have a college degree even to interview with HP. They didn't call their reps salespeople back then, they called them "sales engineers." You can imagine how popular an ambitious young kid with no college degree must have been to some of the people there! But they liked what they saw, and I liked the company. (The way I figured it, any company bright enough to bend the rules to take me on had to have *something* going for it.)

I worked hard and had three stellar years at HP. Then I got cocky and let up a little bit. Guess what happened then. The fourth year rolled around, and I had a very, *very* bad first half.

When I say "bad half," I don't mean that I was a little under quota. I mean I had a *horrendous* half. I was at nineteen percent of quota. I was placed on probation and given a formal memo that was placed in my personnel file. That memo informed me that I had to get my act together within the next six months or I would be fired.

Looking back now, I can see where I went wrong. Slowly but surely, I had stopped prospecting for new business. It happens to a lot of successful salespeople. I was sticking with the old reliables—my existing customer base—and knocking on all the familiar, safe doors. At the rate I was going, there was no way I could support the quota I'd been assigned. (Actually, depending on your existing base to meet *any* quota is a lousy idea. As a general rule, anywhere from seventy-five to ninety percent of your business should come from new business.) I had gradually convinced myself that I could get by with taking shortcuts, and as a result I had nothing, absolutely nothing in the pipeline.

I had six short months to sell enough new computer systems to meet my quota, or I'd be gone.

I finished that year at 103% of quota—and got to keep my job for another year.

■   ■   ■

At the awards banquet, my regional manager came over to shake my hand, which was quite satisfying considering all the pressure I'd been under. He said, "Tony, I have two questions to ask you. The first one is, are these new accounts you sold going to back out after the first of the year?"

I said, "Absolutely not." (And I was right.)

He said, "Okay. The second question is, how the hell did you do it?"

The answer to this question was that I used tactics that I would rely on to this very day. I became less of a salesperson, and more of a businessperson. I began to focus on selling to VITO. I didn't realize it, but my recovery from being put on probation would be the genesis of the book you are holding in your hands.

Think about it. I was in what certainly seemed to be an impossible position. I had to sell maybe half a dozen big new computer systems— not today's PCs, mind you, but high-end, high-priced systems—in *six months*. If you're at all familiar with the computer industry, or any industry that relies on big-ticket sales, you'll realize how tough it is to get large company bureaucracies to requisition a box of blank disks over that period of time, much less approve the purchase of a $250,000 computer system. I *couldn't* go through the standard channels. I had to reach real, live decision makers, people who could say yes or no *instantly* to the ideas I had—and who could actually make things happen within the organization once they realized the potential benefits of my solutions.

I *had* to reach VITO. And I did.

Now, a lot of time has passed since the day I received that awful memo. But you know what? The pressures I faced during that extremely challenging year were not unlike the pressures today's salespeople— and that includes me—face day in and day out. I don't mean to suggest that everyone in sales is failing to meet quota, of course, but I do think it's fair to say that today's salespeople have to produce more, faster, and find more new business than the salespeople of ten or twenty years ago. In effect, today's salespeople are often on an unofficial "permanent probation." They're being told, "Keep us ahead of the competition"

My biggest surprise from that experience with probation was that, after a while, I realized that it was actually *fun* to contact VITOs! All of a sudden I wasn't getting kicked around the parking lot by data processing managers. I was having good conversations with the people at or near the very top of their organization. I was using my time more effectively than ever before. I was finding out who in the company was the right person to get things done in the timeframe I was working under. I was *learning* more about each of the organizations I was contacting than I had ever dreamed possible. And the information was coming from sources I could trust!

And, yes, wonder of wonders, these tactics I developed actually worked. Let me give you an idea of how well they worked. One week, I went so far as to sell a $400,000 computer system by making unannounced visits on my prospects! You read that right. I was selling computer systems worth nearly half a million dollars using new and creative door-to-door cold calling selling tactics.

Now, in answer to the question you're probably asking yourself right now: No, this book is not about sneaking up on decision makers in person when they're not expecting you. And no, door-to-door techniques were not the only way I made it through that year. But the point is, I did make it through—by challenging some cherished assumptions that a lot of salespeople have when it comes to dealing with VITOs. How many do you have?

I know one thing. If I'd stopped to ask my colleagues what they thought about the idea of trying to cold-call on a VITO, I probably never would have made that sale. Fortunately, I was focused enough not to ask. And fortunately, I was focused enough not to listen to my own little voice, which would have told me exactly the same thing!

Tony, you can't walk right in to see VITOs and ask if they want to buy a computer system!

Really?

We're all taught to listen to that little voice. You know what? Sometimes the little voice is right. But most of the time it's self-limiting.

We salespeople spend a lot of time worrying about how to get our foot in the door. And usually we're pretty good at it. But sometimes we need to stop and ask ourselves whether or not the doorway we're sticking our foot into is the right one!

It Worked!

I saved my job! You can't imagine how happy I was about that. (Okay, if you've ever been in a similar situation, maybe you can imagine how happy I was.)

So here's the first pop quiz of the book. What do you think I did after I met the quota that my sales manager, all my colleagues, and even simple common sense said I could never meet? (Okay—*after* I went to Disneyland.) I kept using my new tactics. After the results I had gotten, what else was I going to do? Go back to calling the people at the bottom of the totem pole?

I developed the system, sharpened it, identified what it was that made it work, and turned it into a series of very specific steps and a process for contacting VITOs. That system, which has, of course, evolved over the years, is the subject of this book. And the reason you need to find out about it is that *what I faced that year is now what most of us face every day.* Unless you're selling in a different economy than the one I'm working in, the odds are you simply don't have time to sell the old way any more.

So don't!

Three Groups

The VITOs you'll be dealing with fall into three main categories.

Category one: brand new accounts. More than one sales manager would argue that these accounts are why salespeople exist in the first place. A large part of your job is to get new market share. By selling to

27

VITO, you'll get new business more quickly than ever before—because your focus will be on getting to the most important person in the organization first. You'll start out your sales cycle where it would have ended anyway. And you'll do it a whole lot quicker than you used to, which means your company is going to save money. You'll spend more time with the right accounts, and less time with people and organizations that end up wasting your time.

Category two: in-process opportunities. These are accounts where you've already started your sales work. You've made some progress in the sales cycle. Typically, you're trying to forecast your likelihood of success with this company for your sales manager by assigning a percentage figure to reflect the likelihood that you'll get an order. Even if you call it a fifty-percent account, however, the process seems to drag on for months no matter what you do. Often, you have no idea what's really holding things up. But the sad fact is, you've never met the person ultimately responsible for the decision to award the business. By following this program, you'll be able to feel that you've covered all the bases. You will break the gridlock. The prospect will finally either become a customer or move off your list.

Category three: existing customers. This is where you'll be using the program to solidify loyalty and build a genuine business partnership at a very high level. You won't have to worry anymore about "your" people in the organization being overruled by higher-ups. The highest-up person in the place will *be* your person! And once you earn loyalty at the highest level, the chance of a sudden, unexpected "disconnect" is remote indeed.

■   ■   ■

In the final phase of my career at HP, I was named Most Valuable Player in my region. Talk about satisfaction! A couple of years back I had been called on the carpet and formally told my job was in jeopardy because I was such a lousy salesperson. Now I found myself walking onstage at our year-end meeting and accepting a six-foot-tall trophy commemorating an unbelievable year.

I was able to perform at that level because I perfected my system of reaching top decision makers. I applied it religiously and shared it with other salespeople. You can perform at top levels too, if you consistently apply the same system. That's my promise to you.

Read what follows. *Implement* what follows. Make it yours. Customize it to your environment and your personality. And keep doing it.

■　　■　　■

Have I piqued your interest in this system? I hope so. Keep reading; in the next chapter you'll find out the first and most important thing you must be prepared to do if you want to do business with a VITO.

Chapter Two:
Adding Value to VITO's Day

This part of the book won't take long to read, but it's vitally important. It starts with a simple, powerful idea that is the foundation for everything that follows in this book. Here it comes. Ready?

VITO pays attention to things that *add value to VITO's day*. And not a heck of a lot else.

If you want VITO to pay attention to you, it follows that you will have to find some way to convey the important message that *you can add value*. The problem is, VITO knows from bitter experience that talking with salespeople who don't speak his or her language is a great way to a) hear a lot of empty promises and b) waste time that could be spent doing something more productive. (The sad truth is that we salespeople usually have only ourselves to blame for this state of affairs.) So VITO has learned to spot salespeople, and has come to assume that very few of them are reliable or even vaguely results-oriented when it comes to VITO's interests. As a general rule, VITO is right about this.

Therefore . . .

You must look absolutely, utterly different from any other salesperson VITO has ever encountered. And I'm not talking about wardrobe. I'm talking about personal commitment. When we call on VITO, we're on a job interview. We're proving to VITO that we—not someone else—can offer the best possible solutions. So we must act the part and do anything and everything necessary to build this all-important alliance.

When you get right down to it, *people who are committed to making things happen for VITO* are the ones who earn a spot in his day. You may or may not have something distinctly different from the competition to offer VITO with your product or service, but I can guarantee you that you can come off a heck of a lot more committed to helping VITO run a business successfully than your competitors. You can do this by showing VITO from the very first instant that you are not the average salesperson.

In the end, *you* will make the difference. And you will do it by . . .

Changing Your Focus

The most important thing you will ever do when it comes to earning a spot in VITO's busy schedule is stop being a salesperson.

That's right. This is a book about sales, I run sales seminars all over the country, you're trying to increase your sales performance, and the advice I'm giving you is to stop thinking like a salesperson—and start thinking like a businessperson. A problem-solver. Someone willing to focus on the issues that affect VITO's bottom line. You must, repeat *must* make that transition if you want VITO to take you seriously.

We are talking about changing our style, changing our approach, and changing our attitude. We are talking about changing the way we are perceived. The aim is to be perceived by VITO as more of a businessperson—and less of a salesperson. That means changing vocabulary, changing the way we look at ourselves and our products, services, and solutions, and, perhaps most important, getting out of our world and into VITO's. Remember, VITO has a tough job! Getting a company to meet its goals is no mean feat. We are going to begin focusing on how we can help in this effort. Once we make that transition, the doors to VITO's suite will open.

If you get shunted to a lower level after you have finished reading this book, rest assured that it will be because you have started thinking like a salesperson again. As long as you change your outlook and approach VITO in such a way as to demonstrate that you are a *business ally*, not someone who just wants to "sell VITO something," you will succeed.

At this point in my seminars, someone usually raises a hand and says something like, "Wait a minute, Tony. This all sounds great in theory, but if I put it into practice I'll end up ticking people off! After all, VITO already *has* business allies—the people in the organization, the people I've been calling on! Why on earth would I want to alienate those contacts by going straight to the top?"

What I am going to show you in the chapters that follow is not about going over people's heads or jeopardizing existing contacts. You know and I know that that doesn't work. This system is about professionalism, inclusion, and mutual success for everyone in VITO's organization.

New Accounts, In-Process Accounts, and Current Customers

Whether the focus is on brand new accounts, in-process accounts at which you've already started the sales cycle, or your current customers, in this book we'll look at the best ways to bring VITO into the picture to your (and everyone's) benefit.

My belief is that, in dealing with *any* brand new account, you're much better off going straight to VITO before you talk to anyone else. (It's better to start too high than too low!) I'll be going into the details of how to deal with existing contacts who aren't VITOs later on in the book. For now, though, let me tell you how you're going to win points with people at lower levels when you talk to VITO.

You're going to turn them into heroes in VITO's eyes! And you'll assume all of the risk for them, too.

Of course, getting to that point is going to take some work on your part. Before you can make anyone *else* look good to VITO, you have to be able to make *yourself* look good to VITO. And I'm not going to kid you. You're going to have to make a serious, sustained effort to make this system work, and along the way, you're going to have to become a much better, more competitive businessperson than you've ever been. But you know what? Your career is worth it.

Let's get specific. There are five keys to working with VITO that you will have to master in order to make this book work for you. You can read about them in the next chapter.

CHAPTER THREE:
THE FIVE KEYS
TO WORKING WITH VITO

As promised, here is a summary of the five key qualities you will need to have or develop further if you want to build a businessperson-to-businessperson relationship with VITO.

To Work with VITO
You Will Need Unshakable Confidence

That's unshakable confidence not only in your product, service, or solution, but in yourself as well. How do you develop this? Well, VITOs are pretty similar in their most important qualities. If you learn to deal with one, it's a pretty good bet you'll soon be able to deal with more than one. So . . .

Join Toastmasters. It's a great organization, one that will get you feeling comfortable in front of a whole auditorium full of formerly intimidating decision makers. (And VITOs are birds of a feather, so you're likely to expand your prospect list by attending the meetings.) Toastmasters will be one of the best investments of time you will ever make when it comes to building the confidence necessary to deal with VITOs. So do it.

Go out of your way to deal with the VITOs within your own organization—presidents, executive vice presidents, and the like. When your organization's VITO gives a speech, be sure to attend—and at the end, when he or she asks if there are any questions, *ask a question.* But don't ask just *any* question. Ask a question you've researched for a week and a half, a question that has undeniable relevance to the company's well-being, a question you've practiced in front of the mirror for half an hour or so. And—here's an important technique for dealing with

VITOs—*frame the question in terms of VITO's interests and opinions.* ("VITO, what's important to you about our plan for capturing the Atlantic market with our widgets?") If your office is far-flung, or there is some other obstacle preventing you from meeting with your own organization's VITOs, search out a group that can offer you exposure to VITOs who will not necessarily be sales prospects. The point is not to score points within your own firm (although that's certainly nice), but to become comfortable interacting with VITOs, discussing key points with them, and eliciting their opinions. By the way here's your first helpful hint on meeting with a VITO in person: always take notes, whether or not anything even vaguely important is being said. In actuality, of course, anything and everything a VITO says is important. Write it down and make it obvious that you are doing so.

Join at least one nonprofit organization. Not only will you be adding your efforts to a good cause, you'll meet VITOs! They usually have a strong desire to give something back to the community. (Of course, they also know when something is deductible.) This setting can give you an excellent opportunity to interact with VITOs in a neutral, low-pressure setting. Take advantage of it.

Next, make a point of meeting the VITOs in every one of your current accounts once you've read the later parts of this book on setting up appointments. You may feel that doing this will be easier in some accounts than in others. Fine. Start with the easy ones. You may be nervous about going "over the heads" of your existing contacts. Don't be. You only help your business when you set these appointments up properly—and a little later, we'll be covering exactly how you can arrange things in a way that keeps everyone happy. My bet is that you'll be pleasantly surprised. And, of course, we'll be talking later about referrals to other VITOs; VITOs tend to recommend good companies to other VITOs. How many of your existing accounts should you visit asking to meet with VITO? Only the ones you want to keep. The ones you don't visit will vanish all by themselves.

To Work with VITO
You Must Be Willing to Work to Develop Synergy within Your Organization

That means doing whatever it takes to build a teamwork-first orientation. VITOs know the importance of teamwork these days. We must show VITO that we appreciate the importance of the team, and must demonstrate the effectiveness of our own team. Specifically, you should be willing to:

Give awards or see that your company does. Not just for top salesperson—that award's going to be yours, after all, and you want to spread the wealth around—but for all aspects of contribution to your company's success. Talk to your manager about this if necessary. Trophies and awards have a powerful galvanizing effect on team members. (And by the way, when it's your turn to receive an award, why not take the unforgettable step of engraving the names of other team members who helped you? Don't put the trophy on *your* desk—circulate it to the other team members. Move it around once a month. That's a great way to show those who helped you that you care, and that their efforts are recognized.)

Acknowledge the contributions of others in a public way. At company meetings, mention the help you received from people in production, customer service, or any other applicable area. Give honest and frequent thanks to those who helped to make your success possible. I once received a sales award at a huge company banquet and, as my acceptance speech, simply listed the names of all the people who had helped me to perform at the level I had attained that year. As I mentioned each of their names, I motioned for them to come up onstage with me to take a well-deserved bow. How long do you imagine that gesture was remembered?

To Work with VITO
You Must Be Able to Build Business Rapport

No, you are not being instructed to mirror all of VITO's gestures exactly or breathe in synchronization, two rather simple-minded pieces of advice you will find in many sales-oriented books these days. (For my part, I've always wondered what would happen if two people were following that mirroring advice at the same meeting. Who would be mirroring whom?)

Skip the cute mimicking maneuvers and the transparently ingratiating golf talk. They're usually a waste of everyone's time. Learn how to deal with VITO by:

Making a good first impression with mail, phone, and personal contacts. Your meetings with VITOs are unlike your contacts with any other people. When you meet with most contacts, you are trying to establish a peer or vendor/supplier relationship of some kind. As we mentioned a little earlier, when you meet with VITO for the first time, *you are going on a job interview*, plain and simple—so there is no room for error when it comes to preparation, grooming, and focus. You'll find specific ideas on exactly how to make the most of your first precious few moments of VITO's time in future chapters.

Listening intently. That means listening with undivided attention, focus, and understanding. It means listening with rapt attention. Let me tell you how I first learned about the importance of this. After a tour in the Navy, I began to lose my hearing. Over the years, my hearing got progressively worse. I actually taught myself how to read lips! You know, reading lips is interesting: you really have to concentrate. Your eyes have to be glued to the lips of the person you're talking to, and your mind has to be very focused. You can't daydream. You have to watch every single movement.

Now, back when I was selling large computer systems, I had an interesting experience. I had a number of very important sales meetings with the president of a good-sized company, and I was always right out on the edge of my chair, watching him like a hawk. I'd get as close as I could without getting into the president's personal space. If a distraction took place—if the secretary walked into the office, for instance—I couldn't let the secretary take my attention away. I couldn't afford to miss a single word of what the president had to say.

Throughout those meetings, my eyes and my full attention *belonged* to the president of that company. And I got that sale. I sold his company a fairly large computer system. And you can bet I felt good about it. In part as a reward, I got myself two powerful new hearing aids, almost invisible. As it happened, that president was the very first business contact I met with after I got my hearing aids.

It was great! I could hear everything! I didn't have to lean forward in my chair anymore! I asked the president, "VITO, how's the installation going?" And as VITO started to tell me, guess what happened? I didn't have to look at VITO's lips anymore! Why, I could look around the room! When there was a noise, I could turn to see what it was! When the secretary walked in, I could smile and nod hello!

All of a sudden, the president stopped right in the middle of his sentence. I turned and looked at him. He looked me right in the eye and said, "Tony, take your hearing aids out."

I said, "Why on earth would I want do that?" And he said, "Tony, I feel you're not listening to me. I felt really special before you had those hearing aids. You used to watch every move I made. Please take them out." And I did.

Right then and there I learned one of the most important lessons in my sales career: When you're with a prospect, you listen to them as if you're hard of hearing! Listen to them as though you must read their lips. Give them your undivided attention. Show them you are interested in understanding how they feel. Listen with empathy.

Forget about closing. Now if this isn't a departure from standard sales, advice, nothing is! You read right. I want you to commit yourself to *never meeting with VITO with the intention of closing a deal.* News flash: VITOs don't like "being closed." Think about it. You probably don't like it either. You are not *closing* doors, but *opening* them. You are working to develop an ongoing business relationship for which you will always be willing to take ultimate responsibility. Remove the word "closing" from your vocabulary. Just go out and open relationships and business opportunities. When you get VITO's first order, it's the beginning, not the end.

To Work with VITO
You Must Have an Unlimited Desire to Succeed

And you know what? I can't give you this. I can, however, share some of my own feelings on the subject and give you some idea of the degree of commitment to personal success required if you want to deal with VITO.

Remember that the first time is hard—but follow-through takes guts, too. Let me give you a perfect illustration of this. I was conducting a seminar in the Northeast once; there was a young man named Scott who sat right up in front, took copious notes, and paid rapt attention throughout. I later learned that, very early on the Monday morning following this seminar, this rep went into his office, picked up the phone, and started calling VITOs in his territory. The director of sales happened to notice him making the calls.

Later on that day, the director walked into his little cubicle. Now you have to picture this: he was sitting down, and the director of sales, who's rather a big man, was standing up. The director of sales said, "I noticed you in here early this morning making calls. Are you doing that stuff that you learned at Tony's seminar last week?" Scott looked up and said, "Yeah, I'm giving it a try." The director of sales said, "Well? How's it going? Are you getting through to any VITOs?"

"Yeah," he answered. "I just got through to the president of a big company." The director of sales grinned broadly. "So?" he asked. "How did the call turn out?"

Scott looked at the floor and said, "I got so nervous I hung up on him."

Can you imagine that? Now, I'll grant you, it's not always going to be easy. But if you follow the program and follow through as I suggest, you will become more familiar with it in time—and your confidence will increase.

By the way, there's a happy end to the story. When this incident took place, that rep was in serious trouble—just a little over halfway to his first-quarter quota, not a good place to be in early spring. He kept at it. He wasn't satisfied with the result he got the first time out, so he summoned up the mental energy to come back, change the approach a little bit, and try again. Scott closed the year at 240% of quota!

Do you think he would have posted those results if he'd given up after the very first try? Of course not!

Look at everything as a result. If you're not happy with a result, you take the right steps to change it. If, when you try to change it, you find that it gets a little bit worse, don't panic! You know now not to try to change it in that direction. Keep at it.

Hate the word failure. I do, and I simply refuse to admit it into my day. I have setbacks, disguised opportunities, and new selling environments. But I do not have failures until I give up the idea of learning from my experiences, and I never, ever do that. Ditto for the words no, rejection, slump, or anything else that removes selling power and authority from you and places it somewhere else.

To Work with VITO
You Must Have Unlimited Energy

And that's not just physical energy, but mental energy as well. I'm talking about determination on top of determination. Streetfighters know that the most formidable opponents are not always the biggest ones, but the ones who leap right back up fiercer than ever after you've knocked them down. *That's* trouble. Without for a minute losing sight of the fact that our relationship with VITO is based on mutual benefit and mutual victory in a business setting, we also have to remember that getting over the barriers and into VITO's office takes staying power. Fortunately, VITOs, above all other businesspeople, know the value of persistence— and appreciate it. If all else fails . . .

Remember the space shuttle. Did you know that 50% of the fuel stored in those huge tanks strapped onto the bottom of the space shuttle is expended just to get 1,000 yards off the launch pad? It's true. And that's just the way it is with VITO. Half of your energy is going to be expended initiating the relationship. Once you get over that hump, you and VITO will be riding to the stars and back again.

When you partially accomplish a goal, reward yourself with a little of the reward you've got planned for attaining the entire goal. Let's say you hit your targets for each month of a quarter—and you've just been named Salesperson of the Quarter by your manager. Treat yourself, in some small way, as if you had achieved your yearly quota! As long as you are on target to achieve your yearly goal, do something special as a reward to yourself—something you would normally associate with the reward you will receive for attaining your yearly goal. If you planned a ski vacation, for instance, you might decide to take a long weekend to visit the slopes. If you do something like this throughout the course of the year, you will feel as though you've *already* made your goals for the year. In most cases, this will instill you with a sense of confidence—not complacency. Visualization is good, but actually *experiencing* a partial reward you associate with your yearly goal can work wonders, too.

For my part, I'm always chasing a goal. Last year, I promised myself that if I made my yearly revenue goals, I'd buy myself a new Jaguar. Halfway through the year, I was on target—so rather than wait until the end of the year, I took the opportunity to reward myself for my good work by *renting* a Jaguar for a week. I loved it! In fact, I so hated giving it up at the end of the week that I was *supremely* motivated to hit my targets for the remaining two quarters. And I did!

(By the way, my Jaguar convertible is French vanilla with a blue cloth top. It does 140 miles per hour. Or so I'm told.)

■   ■   ■

So much for the profile of the businessperson who can get through to VITO. What about VITO's profile? It's time to take a close look at the person you'll be building this new business relationship with.

Chapter Four:
A Portrait of VITO

Who is VITO?

VITO is the person who can make your sale happen (or take your sale away from you), regardless of what anyone else has to say about it.

Simple, isn't it? VITO is the person with the ultimate power, influence, and authority to make things happen in an organization, even if everyone else in that organization disagrees with a particular decision. As we pointed out earlier, VITO has the ultimate veto power. VITO can stop something from happening even if everyone else in the organization says "yes"; VITO can make something happen even though everyone else in the organization says "no."

VITOs are CEOs, presidents, chairpersons of the board. Sometimes VITOs have what appear to be less-than-all-encompassing titles (executive vice president, for instance), but still fit the definition because *even people technically above them on the flow chart do not proceed with a course of action if they perceive that VITO objects to it*. We are concerned with the real world here, not with formal hierarchies. If the president of a company has difficulty making decisions, runs every meaningful decision past the vice president of operations for "input," and always follows that vice president's recommendations, then the VP, not the president, is your real VITO.

As a general rule, there is one VITO per organization or division. They fly alone. Just as flocks of eagles are pretty rare sights, you don't often see a flock of VITOs.

As demanding and intimidating as they can sometimes appear to be, VITOs are people too. They are still subject to essentially the same factors that govern just about every other human being on the planet. They want to maximize pleasures, rewards, and satisfactions; they want to minimize errors, waste, and other setbacks. They want to do the best they can by their companies, their shareholders, their customers, their employees, and their families. They also have a great many responsibilities, of course, and they've learned a lot and developed the ability to make shrewd judgments over the years. They're often quite tough to convince. But if they can find a way to do things better, more effectively—without committing what their experience tells them is likely to be a mistake or taking an unnecessary risk—they will do so.

Now, a good many salespeople have learned over the years exactly what it takes to talk a good game. And a good many salespeople are so removed from what customers actually experience with their products and services that they develop, knowingly or unknowingly, a severe credibility gap with top decision makers in general—and VITOs in particular.

So if your aim is to keep sounding like a standard salesperson, or to leave the actual execution of your promises to someone else in your organization whose work you don't have to worry about—guess what? VITOs will simply have no patience for you. They may have resigned themselves to the fact that their organization will have to do business with those kinds of salespeople from time to time, but they *will not* take calls from them if they can possibly avoid doing so, and they certainly won't agree to any appointments.

On the other hand, VITOs *enjoy* getting calls from other businesspeople who have new ideas—and will decide to meet with them and do business with them if they feel it is in their best interest to do so. You have your doubts about this? Don't. I promise you, this principle has been borne out time and time again—by me and by thousands upon thousands of others. The general rule of thumb seems to be that if you have three new valid, workable ideas, VITO will agree to meet with you. Believe it. But the key is, VITO must perceive that these ideas are coming from someone of *Equal Business Stature*.

That's a terribly important point, so important that I'm going to ask you to forgive me for repeating it. VITO must perceive that the ideas you are proposing are coming from someone of *Equal Business Stature*. No, that doesn't mean you must have an equal business *title*. If that were the case, only a company president could talk to another company president, and you have my word that nothing could be further from the truth than that. What I mean is that when you call VITO, you have to communicate as one professional businessperson to another.

If what you have to say and the way you say it sounds like it's coming from the basic, run-of-the-mill, get-the-signature-and-don't-worry-about-any-follow-up sales rep, forget it. VITO will hang up—fast. But if VITO senses that the person on the other end of the line is a businessperson who is responsible for actually making things happen and delivering results, you will be able to find an opening.

I want you to have Equal Business Stature with VITO. Now, you don't have an equal business *title* with VITO, but that's okay. You don't need it.

What do I mean by Equal Business Stature? I mean that you should have an *understanding of VITO's problems* and a new idea for some possible solutions to those problems. If you can show VITO that, you will have Equal Business Stature. And when you have that, VITO will spend time with you.

Let me underscore the importance of building Equal Business Stature—and, in so doing, making the effort to understand what VITOs face every day. Once you commit to this, you will have effectively moved out of that "salesperson" category and into the "businessperson" category. And that's what this program is all about!

If you take only one idea away from this chapter, it should be what we have just reviewed: VITO prefers to talk to people of Equal Business Stature, and by that I mean people who understand problems and have ideas for solving them. I mean people who are committed to delivering results and are willing to be held accountable for them. (As a matter of fact, it's a good bet that, on any given day, VITO will talk *only* to people who fall into this category.)

At this stage of the training I give, many salespeople feel a greater gap than ever opening up between themselves and the VITOs they know they will have to try to contact. Don't panic yet! Let's look in a little more detail at some of VITO's typical characteristics. I'm willing to bet you'll be pleasantly surprised.

VITO in a Nutshell

VITO's titles include . . .
  Chief executive officer
  President

Vice president
Chief financial officer
Owner
Partner
Board member
Executive vice president

VITO's key characteristics are . . .
Leadership
Credibility
Passion
Vision
Understanding of the "big picture"
Strong ego
Emphasis on power, control, and authority
Decisiveness
Creativity
Openness to new ideas
Willingness to take calculated risks

VITO's agenda and favorite business discussion topics are . . .
Leading-edge success for the company and VITO
The company's image and what it stands for
How to define the company's mission statement
The team and the product
Keeping ahead of competitors
Measurable, tangible results (the bottom line)

VITO wants to see results like . . .
Increased revenues, stock prices, market share, and prestige
Reduced expenses
New edge on the competition
Reduced time to market

For VITO, victory means . . .
A winning organization admired by all
Being recognized as a leader by both industry and community

Gaining greater power and control

Now, What about *Your* VITO?

What you just saw was my summary of the VITOs I've come in contact with. That's good for you to know, but it's not as important as the characteristics of the VITOs *you're* likely to run into. On a separate piece of paper, jot down the important facts about a VITO you know. Although it's best to profile a VITO from an organization you have either sold to or plan to sell to, you don't have to do that. If you want, you can write about the head of your own organization.

Your profile should include:

- VITO'S name and title
- VITO's key characteristics
- VITO's agenda and favorite business discussion topics
- VITO's desired results
- VITO's definition of victory

■   ■   ■

Do you notice anything interesting about the profiles of VITO we've been examining in this chapter?

VITO has many of the qualities of a successful salesperson! If you were to list your own personality traits, my bet is that you would find that you share some very important characteristics with the people who head up companies. After all, a good many VITOs *began their careers in sales*. In other words, they know good (and bad) sales work when they see it.

So you must show VITOs the good work. Make it obvious that you are willing to share new ideas and stand behind them.

At the end of the day, you're likely to find that you have a lot more in common with VITO than you'd first imagined.

Results

I can't emphasize enough that VITOs are big on making things happen. Another way to phrase this is that they have strong *result orientation.* Tangible results that VITOs like to see—and quantify—might include:

- Increasing efficiency
- Lowering the cost of sales
- Raising revenues
- Increasing repeat customer rates
- Attracting new customers
- Increasing market share
- Lowering expenses
- Getting higher dividends
- Decreasing the downtime of revenue-producing employees
- Getting products to market quicker than the competition does
- Keeping shareholders happy
- Lowering workmen's comp claims

There are intangibles, too. For instance:

- Being the supreme leader
- Having a good personal image
- Having a good company image
- Retaining happy employees who stay late and come in early

And so on. But the key for VITOs is results; these people are big on specific, demonstrable progress and measurable results.

Please reread that list of *tangible* benefits I just outlined. Now ask yourself: Does your product or service do any of those things? Of course—otherwise you wouldn't be in business!

■   ■   ■

So. That's VITO. Now, then. Who else will you be dealing with?

CHAPTER FIVE:
OTHER PLAYERS IN THE DRAMA—AND THE INFLUENCE AND AUTHORITY NETWORK

In addition to VITO, of course, there are a number of other people who populate the offices and hallways of the typical business or organization. For our purposes, there are three more categories; we'll be looking at them in this chapter. One in particular is likely to be pretty familiar to you.

Every company you call on has a four-step network of people with surprisingly different levels of influence and authority regarding purchasing decisions. No surprise: VITO is at the top. But you should also be able to categorize others in the organization according to the breakdown we'll be examining in a moment, which I call the *Influence and Authority Network*.

You may be asking yourself what I mean by influence and authority—and how these things affect the way an organization works.

As I use the term in this book, influence means "having the ability to change the minds of others, especially those in high places." And authority means "having the power to make decisions and the control to spend money." VITOs, of course, outrank everyone else on the chart in these two categories. But there is a distinct hierarchy beneath the top level that you should be aware of, as well.

Managers and Directors

These people are one step below VITO. They're the ones who take the vision VITO has defined and turn it into workable policy objectives. They translate the mission statement into a series of instructions and initiatives for others in the organization to follow. In short, they're the people who march the troops toward the goals defined by VITO.

Managers and directors have fairly high levels of influence and authority—but not, of course, as much as VITO.

Intellects (or "Seymours")

One step below the managers and directors you will find the intellects, the all-important advisors to the managers. I also call them "Seymours" because they always, *always* want to "see more" data, demonstrations, presentations, flip-charts, and full-color regression analyses. My guess is that, if you've been in sales for more than a month or so, you have spent more than your share of time with various Seymours (who, like VITOs, come in both genders). Seymours poke holes in proposals. Seymours want you to provide lots and lots of charts and samples and spreadsheets and full-color animated scenarios before they will even consider committing to anything. Very often, they will refuse to commit to anything after you have supplied them with enough truckloads of information and samples to alter the earth's gravitational balance.

Seymours look at solutions in terms of technical capabilities to fit their *real or perceived* needs. Often, of course, for all their expertise, Seymours have a skewed perspective that derails proposals that can be of real benefit to the organization.

Seymours have lots of influence (which, given their distaste for decision making, is another way of saying that they spend a great deal of time shooting things down). They typically have very limited authority; they are not movers and shakers within the organization.

Consumers

No, these are not the *organization's* customers; these are the people who will actually use what you are selling, the ones who carry out the policies of the managers as per the specifications of the Seymours. These are the worker bees; they have little or no authority and very limited influence—unless, of course, they are related to VITO!

Before you dismiss this group altogether, however (as many salespeople do), you should remind yourself that these people know a lot about the organization they work for—and knowledge is power, especially when it comes to dealing with VITOs. And getting information from a consumer carries the not-insignificant advantage that doing so does not run the risk of stalling your attempt to reach VITO! So your relationship with the word processing worker or warehouse person may be a good deal more important than you think.

The Influence and Authority Network

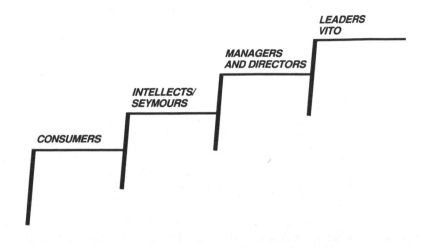

At this point in my seminar, someone usually points out that a good many VITOs pride themselves on seeing things from the point of view of their employees, and may actually be so brazen as to make a habit of fielding calls on the 800 line customers use to call in and file complaints.

So—can a VITO also be a consumer?

The answer is, Yes, if you are selling something VITO will be using—but that doesn't really change the landscape that much. Managers and Seymours may decide to become members of the group or groups *below* them—but never above. In other words, VITO may be a consumer, but a consumer can't be VITO.

As a matter of fact, VITO can be in any of the other three categories, or all four at once! But the key thing to keep in mind is that, while VITO may decide to wear every hat, *no one else in the organization can do this!*

51

Another question salespeople often have at this stage has to do with that hard-to-categorize title, vice president. Does the VP automatically fall into the manager category? There is no definitive answer, because the most important factor is not what the VP is *called*, but what he or she *does*. If the VP drives the company's sales and marketing efforts and can veto the decisions of others in that area, it's a pretty good bet that she's a VITO. (Remember, though, that there is usually one and only one supreme mover and shaker in an organization or division.)

Usually, when referring to VITO, I use the term "president" because it's easiest that way. However, the president of an organization may well be a figurehead, someone whose main function in life is to shake the hands of shareholders and employees. You're interested in identifying the person with *ultimate influence and authority*. In a municipality, that might be the treasurer. In a law firm, that might be the senior partner. Focus on functions, responsibility, power, and authority, not titles.

VITO Power

So let's review what we know. VITO has the ultimate "Yes" power, and the power to veto the decisions of others in the Influence and Authority Network. Regardless what you know about the organization, and regardless of any efforts on your part, you can rest assured that VITO will become *very* involved in the decision to buy your solution *if* any of the following conditions exist.

1. Your solution is likely to have an impact on the way VITO's organization interacts with its customers, and VITO knows it.

2. The economy in general or VITO's industry in particular is in a state of flux, and VITO knows that what you are offering will make a transition period easier.

3. Your solution crosses departmental or divisional lines.

4. Your solution will definitely have a significant impact on company revenues or expenses, and VITO knows it.

5. Your product, service, or solution represents a change in source of supply, *and* one or more of the other four situations I have just outlined exists.

Of course, sometimes it's not so apparent to us that VITO is involved with our sales. But you can bank on the general principles I've just outlined.

Why not take a moment now to write down, on a separate piece of paper, the instances in which VITOs in your accounts have become involved with your sales. Do they parallel the reasons I have set out above?

■　■　■

Of course, VITO will be more *directly* involved in the decision to buy from you when you call on VITO first. Doing that empowers you and allows you to shorten your sales cycle—because VITO sees the big picture! (That's part of VITO's job, remember?) VITO will, repeat, *will* understand the importance of the solution you are offering—if you only take the time and trouble to communicate what you have to offer in such a way that it addresses the items on VITO's agenda.

CHAPTER SIX:
THE SEYMOUR PROBLEM

Consumers and managers are important players within the organiza-
tion, and we may even have some experience in dealing with them.
For most of us, however, the sales cycle begins—and, all too often,
drags on and on before coming to an inglorious end—with Seymour,
the intellect.

Sometimes I'm accused of being a little too hard on Seymours—or
intellects, as I sometimes call them—and I imagine there's probably
some truth to that accusation. So before we go any further, let me explain something. My own mother-in-law, a dear woman whom I love
and who works closely with me, is a true-blue intellect. She's played a
very important part in the development and growth of my business, precisely because she can tackle the tough, analytical problems that come
up so often. Intellects play a tremendously important role in just about
any organization you care to name. The problem is that we as salespeople tend not to realize exactly how they fit into the chain of command. Accordingly, we're often frustrated when we try to work with
them. But the problem is usually ours, not theirs.

I've found, from personal experience, that good salespeople tend
to work better with VITOs than they do with Seymours. That doesn't mean
that Seymours aren't likable, hard-working professionals. It just means that,
for our purposes, we're better off trying to contact VITO directly.

What's in a Name?
This is important. Sometimes Seymour goes by a fancy name like
"Manager of Data Processing" or "Senior Executive Human Resource
Development Coordinator." Again, you should not be fooled by titles.
If a contact is an advisor, a tester, a looker-around-corners first and
foremost, that contact is a Seymour.

Mistaking a Seymour for a manager or director is a common mistake that will stall your sales cycle, your progress toward your quota, and your career!

Seymour in a Nutshell

Seymour's titles typically include . . .
>Analyst
>Systems manager
>MIS manager
>Engineering manager
>Consultant
>>(Consultants are usually, but not always, prime Seymour candidates. Accordingly, they are usually, but not always, loathed by salespeople. By the way, have you ever noticed how consultants get in the door by promising to be objective, then simply recommend the products of the company they used to work for? Could there be a connection there?)
>Telecommunications manager
>Accounting supervisor
>Buyer
>Purchasing agent
>Plant manager
>Office manager
>Head accountant

Seymour's key characteristics are . . .
>Technical background; almost always formally educated, and often serves as "backbone" of company on complex technical issues
>Loves to find problems and solve them
>Is focused on job at hand
>Is security-minded
>Is loyal to current source of supply
>Doesn't like to make decisions or take risks
>Always wants to see more data

Seymour's agenda and favorite business discussion topics are . . .
>Techno-facts: features, functions, figures, and future products
>How your technical solutions fit Seymour's real or perceived needs
>How your solution actually works and what will happen if it doesn't

Seymour wants to see results like . . .
> Accumulation of knowledge as power
> The most correct, perfect, zero-defect solution possible

For Seymour, victory means . . .
> Getting the best performance for the price
> An ever-increasing skill and knowledge base
> Recognition as the ultimate problem-solver
> Continuous job security
> Knowing more about products and technology than a salesperson
> > (sound familiar?)

Now, What about *Your* Seymour?

If you've been selling for any period of time, you've probably run into more Seymours than you care to remember. Nevertheless, I want you to take a moment now to profile a Seymour who seems to you to be most typical of the kind you run into. Again, it's not *my* observations on Seymour that will make the difference for you, but your own knowledge base of how Seymours act in the industry you're selling to.

Think of a Seymour you know. Now, on a separate sheet of paper, list:

- SEYMOUR'S name and title
- SEYMOUR'S key characteristics
- SEYMOUR'S agenda and favorite business discussion topics
- SEYMOUR'S desired results
- SEYMOUR'S definition of victory

Some Further Observations on Seymours

Let's review what we have.

For one thing, Seymours don't like making decisions.

This is a defining characteristic of Seymours the world over, and the trait that most frequently drives to distraction the salespeople who come their way.

Seymours are analytical; they don't like taking risks; and they love to gather information. It's not surprising then that they feel there is a right or wrong answer for any situation. (A side note: It's been estimated that college graduates take over 2,600 tests by time they get their degree! Most of them look for right and wrong answers when confronted with something new. Seymours are usually quite well educated and *nearly always* look at things in an on-off, right-wrong way. If you don't have the right answer for a Seymour, you'd better be able to explain why.)

Seymours have tunnel vision—they usually attack one job at a time. They are loyal (often fiercely so). They are impressed by binges, although not always by increased efficiency. They have little or no tolerance for change; they are security-minded and zealously guard their interests against perceived threats.

Seymours love technology—especially if they're they only ones who can get a particular piece of it to do something. In general, though, we have to remember that Seymours are *risk-averse*. They'd like to be the first (and, perhaps, only) person on the block to get the new model Z— but not if doing so will expose them to what they perceive as unjustifiable gambles.

This brings us to an interesting dynamic. Typically, your aim is to highlight ways *the prospect's company* can increase its efficiency. Often, though, these ways will infringe on Seymour's monopoly on an existing, and inefficient, technology! Less equipment? How will Seymour fill the day? This phenomenon—technology as a symbol of empire, rather than as a means of attaining a company objective—represents yet another reason you must be willing to present your solutions initially to VITO!

Seymours are the ones who never seem to take a vacation. They're afraid something might change when they're gone.

Seymours are often thin-skinned. They don't take criticism well.

Seymours may be tinkerers. "Can we take the top panel off this thing and look inside?" (Engineers are often the most influential Seymours in an organization.) They will talk facts, features, and functions (the "F words" beloved by Seymours the world over) all day long if you let them.

Who Does This Sound Like?

Well, like any number of contacts you've encountered over the course of your career. But the salient point is, the person we've just described *doesn't* sound like he or she could do what you do for a living. How many things do you as a salesperson have in common with Seymour? My bet is that, if you have been earning your living as a salesperson for more than a month or so, there are very few.

Just take a moment and think of some people in your company or department who didn't work out as salespeople. I'm talking about people who had to leave due to income problems, or who were fired, or who simply decided they weren't cut out for your line of work. Didn't one or two of them remind you of Seymour? Many of these characteristics (intolerance for change, inability to take criticism, and tunnel vision, to name only a few) are ones that would spell certain doom for anyone pursuing a career in sales. And yet . . .

And yet Seymours are our most common contact in an organization, aren't they?

Picture this. Seymour is at home one evening reading *Scientific American* and, at the same time, watching the Discovery Channel. Seymour's kid walks in the room and says, "I know what I want to be when I grow up!" Seymour puts down the magazine and presses the mute button on the remote, looks at the kid, and says, "Oh? What?" And the kid says, "I want to be a salesperson."

Can't you just picture Seymour bolting out of that easy chair, looking to the heavens, and asking, "God, please tell me—where did I go wrong?"

We have very little if anything in common with Seymour. We have all sorts of things in common with VITO. (And note that, while we may think of *closing* sales with Seymours, we always *open* relationships with VITOs.)

The Seymour Trap in a Nutshell

We recognize the portrait of Seymour in an instant, and there's a reason. Seymour's personality quirks and professional foibles are almost universally accepted as part of the territory the average salesperson must master. If you doubt it, think of the sales managers you've worked with. Most sales managers spend the majority of their time talking their salespeople through problems with various Seymours.

Seymour is the one (or so we tell ourselves) whom we must somehow convince to come down on our side despite all of those analytical digressions; the one we have to cajole into issuing a recommendation in our favor by providing more colorful charts, more detailed reports, more exhaustive surveys; the one we must bury with an avalanche of information so thorough and so detailed that not a single one of those finely honed problems, questions, and skepticisms will be left standing. We assume that if we can only give Seymour what he or she wants and then some, we will, we must, eventually get a decision.

Without exploring the validity of these assumptions, let's look for a moment at a separate issue. Isn't it interesting that we salespeople spend so much of our time talking to Seymours, who have, as we have seen, so little in common with us?

Why do you suppose we do that?

Well, one major reason is that Seymours, unlike VITOs, are usually relatively easy to get to. In fact, most of them *love* meeting with salespeople. But do you know why that is? They want us to do their work for them! All too often, Seymours schedule appointments with us because they know we are willing to give them a free education!

We set up all the meetings: all the graphs, all the charts, all the tests, all the reviews. We summarize everything as neatly as a well-organized encyclopedia. And then we watch as Seymour takes the business somewhere else. If we win over two or two and a half Seymours out of ten in this way, maybe we call it a good quarter. But is it really?

Seymour is easy to reach. So we spend a huge portion of our typical day—of our year, of our *career*—in discussions with Seymour, who would never dream of being a salesperson, and with whom we have very little in common. VITO is hard to reach. So we spend little if any time with VITO, with whom we have almost *everything* in common.

What's wrong with this picture?

So Long, Seymour!

Seymours have their place in the world and in your prospect organization, but for your purposes Seymour should be regarded as *someone you will turn into a hero in VITO's eyes* and nothing more. If you haven't yet gotten religion and concluded that you *must* avoid Seymour at all costs in your initial contacts with a new organization, and *must* instead attempt to contact VITO, go back to Square One and reread the chapters of this book that precede this one.

"But Seymour Is an Important Source of Information!"

So claim many (indeed, most) of the salespeople I have worked with. My response is a concise one requiring only one word, a rejoinder that can, for the purposes of this book, be euphemistically rendered as "baloney."

Of the four major players in the organization, Seymour is hands down the *worst* source of information you can appeal to. There are three reasons for this.

1. They don't mind misleading you. Seymours are the least likely people in the organization to be honest with you on matters of importance.

2. Seymours are often unaware of important new business initiatives in the organization, initiatives that managers, VITOs, and even informed consumers may know about. (Consumers, we must remember, often keep an ear out for gossip or have special contacts with key people in the organization.)

3. Seymours are the most likely people in the organization to use an "exchange" of information with you on a "confidential" basis as a means of obtaining facts that will then be relayed directly to your competition.

You may feel some skepticism on these points, and if you do, you're not alone. Many, many salespeople have, after years of developing a comfortable set of habits in dealing with Seymours, allowed themselves the luxury of a few myths regarding these "allies" within the organization. So let me address each of the points I've just made in a little more detail.

The most important reason not to make your first substantive contact in the organization with someone you know or suspect to be a Seymour is that *Seymour will mislead you about important issues.* You may feel perfectly comfortable, for instance, asking Seymour to tell you who is in charge of making the final decision to purchase a particular product or service your company offers. This is a serious error, and if you're really honest about your own contacts with Seymours you'll understand why. Seymour will *virtually always* tell you that he, Seymour, is the person totally responsible for making that purchasing decision, and this is rarely (if ever) the case!

Remember: Seymours jealously guard their territory within the organization. And they love to set aside an afternoon to pick the brains of salespeople. So why not tell you they're the ones who "handle that," or who must "approve" your proposals, or are "heading up a group" dealing with your product or service? Why not tell you that they will be making the final decision?

As a whole, Seymours are insular types who tend to focus on the project in front of them rather than the big picture. (If they were good at focusing on the big picture, they'd have graduated to the manager level!)

Finally, you should avoid contacting Seymours for information because they often "shoot the breeze" with you, take information you have provided on the (spoken or unspoken) hope that it is to be used only within that organization, and then drop key bits of information about *your firm's* plans, prices, or suppliers into a conversation with the sales rep who is the current supplier. If this has never happened to you, then you live in a different universe from the one in which I sell.

Now, it is true that this is a potential danger with persons who *aren't* Seymours. But it is much *less* of a danger with, say, managers, simply because of the sheer volume of contact Seymour has with salespeople in general and is likely to have with your competitors in particular. If *you're* calling Seymour, it's a good bet *they'll* be calling Seymour. (Of course, having read this chapter, you should now be more than willing to let them do so! After all, the primary virtue of a blind alley is that it exists for a rival to walk down.)

■　　■　　■

"So How *Do* I Make the First Contact?"

So much for why to avoid Seymour. If you're like most of the salespeople I've worked with, right about now you're asking yourself exactly how you're supposed to go about tracking down VITOs and getting meetings. What's the secret? Wash their car? Show up at their daughter's birthday party? Find out their favorite candy and burst into the office with an open box?

The actual technique is much simpler, and will not, I promise, require that you do anything absurd in public or private. All you have to do is write a letter, a letter unlike any you've ever seen or written. The first steps—the research steps—are outlined a little later in the book. In the next chapter, we'll look at your objectives during your first contact with each category of worker in VITO's organization.

I'll take this opportunity to remind you that the road to building a business relationship with VITO is not easy, not standard, and certainly not what you're used to when it comes to "contacting decision-makers." But the techniques we'll be looking at in the next few chapters (techniques that, I want to remind you, I personally use on a daily basis) *will* pay handsome dividends . . . and will help you initiate a genuine long-term alliance with the most important person in the organization.

Chapter Seven:
Call Objectives

I've got a friend named Dean who's the president of a huge trading company. Going to his office is like taking a trip around the world. He's got artifacts from all over. One side of his office is taken up with a huge map of the world, with all the company's factories and processing plants and ships marked with color pictures. As the ships move across the ocean, Dean plots their progress.

I always get to Dean's office early when we have a lunch appointment, which is about once a month. One day, I was sitting outside in the reception area when Joyce, the secretary, said, "Go ahead and have a seat in Dean's office. He's on the phone, but he won't mind if you go in. Just be quiet—he's right in the middle of a big negotiation."

This guy has three phones on his desk. Each phone has 4 buttons. As I walk in, most of those 12 buttons seem to be flashing. Dean has a big legal pad in front of him; he's punching away at an adding machine; he's doing a lot of complicated calculations.

Dean picks up one line. "Harry! Thirty-three five? Okay. Hold." He punches a button, puts the phone on the hook, scribbles something, then punches a different button and picks up the receiver again. "Hey, George. Thirty-eight five? Okay. Hold."

He goes through this routine a couple of times, lights blinking and numbers crunching. He reaches a moment when he has to take a deep breath. I say, "Dean, what's going on?" Dean jumps out of his chair, walks over to the map on the wall, and points to a ship off the coast of Central America.

Dean says, "Tony, this ship is loaded with mesquite." (That's the kind of wood you use for barbecues.) "I'm looking for the highest price; I'm having a bidding conference on the phone. There are 9 people bidding for that shipload."

"Dean," I say, "why don't you put all these people on one line? Put them all on your speakerbox. Then have an auction. You know how it is in an auction—the fever really gets going, and you'd probably get a better price."

"Can you do that right now?" Dean asks.

Well, I assure Dean that I can, and within thirty seconds I'm working with his assistant to set up the conference call. I show my little telephone credit card to Joyce and say, "Call this 800 number and tell the operator you want to have a teleconference with all these people." Eight minutes later, Dean is no longer sitting in front of a pad. He's standing up. He's walking around his office. He's got six people on the phone, all of them bidding for that shipload of mesquite. The price keeps going higher and higher and finally closes at fifty. (To this day, I don't know if that's fifty Krugerrands, fifty thousand dollars, or fifty cents per metric ton.)

After everyone hangs up, there's one more light flashing on Dean's bank of phones. He picks up that line and says, "Arturo? Liverpool." He was talking to the captain of the ship!

Then I ask Dean, "What does it cost to have that ship waiting around for you to tell it where to go?" Dean answers, "Tony, you don't want to know. Hey, where can I get one of those cards?"

Just for the sake of argument, let's pretend that it was my job to sell long-distance phone service. What would I have just done?

Well, I created Equal Business Stature with Dean, for one thing. First, I showed him that I understood a problem he had. Then I presented a new idea for a solution. And I phrased it in the form of a benefit when I pointed out to Dean that he could get a better price for his goods by holding a real live phone auction. When I showed Joyce how to use my card, I took on the role of the consumer by showing her how to use the service. If I had called on Seymour, I might have had to show him how many lines the service could accommodate in the event all twenty-one of Dean's lines had been blinking at the same time, explained the system's use of fiber-optic technology, and examined a dozen other techno-facts. And if I had called on one of Dean's managers, I would have had to describe how the long-distance service would have presented a unique advantage for that manager's department or the organization as a whole by describing the various service options and advantages.

Each player in VITO's organization speaks a different language.

In your contacts with each, you must be able to speak the proper language.

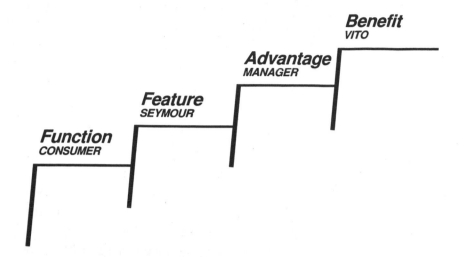

Now, as I mentioned earlier, the way you're going to enter VITO's world is by sending a letter. That may seem a little old-fashioned in today's fax-driven, phone-driven business environment, but it works. Surprise! The much-maligned Postal Service is going to be one of the ways you'll introduce yourself to the VITOs you identify.

But don't start tapping on your computer yet! You can't just send any old letter to VITO, and you can't stick it in any old envelope. As you know, an endless barrage of unexpected mail hits VITO's office daily. Your first goal is to *stand out from that traffic.* If you don't do that, all is lost. One way to do that is to pay close attention to the physical packaging of your message, and this is something we'll be addressing a little later in the book. Another way is to do a little research before you compose the letter. But the bottom-line *best* way to stand out from those competing messages is to speak VITO's language. And before we can begin crafting that all-important letter, we'll have to look at the principle by which VITOs judge all attempts to communicate with them, written or otherwise.

As we've seen in the story I told about Dean, that principle is simple and can be summarized in two questions VITO will ask about what you have to say: *Does this benefit me? If so, how?*

Different Messages for Different People—and Pre-Letter Requests for Information

Let me underscore this vitally important point: Each of the types of workers in VITO's organization has a different objective in dealing with you. You will need to highlight different aspects of your product, service, or solution in your dealings with each of them.

- Consumers need to know about *functions*. They will be concerned with how to make your solution function properly, how you will help them do their jobs. Envision consumers as the end-users who must be able to work better as a result of your solution.

- Seymours need to know about *features*. That means what each component of your solution does, how all the parts and elements interact, what gives your solution its character. Seymours need to know why what you are proposing is needed. Think of Seymour looking "under the hood" to inspect all the component parts and characteristics of what you have to offer.

- Managers and directors need to know about *advantages*. They want to know what your solution will do for the department, whether what you have to offer provides a leading-edge advantage that helps the department achieve the company's mission statement.

- VITOs need to know about *benefits*. They want to know how your solution will help the company realize its fullest potential and what bottom-line results can be expected.

Depending on your own circumstances, you may decide that some kind of research call preceding the letter we're about to draft is necessary. In some cases you will need to make a trip to the library, read an annual report, or gather information from a conversation with a consumer or manager within the organization.

Here's an important piece of advice. If you need information on a company, contact the company's sales rep! Your call will get right through or will be returned almost immediately. Nine times out of ten, you will get everything you want to know: VITO's name, the firm's competitors, any problems with the current service—it's really up to you.

Don't quiz the receptionist, whose job it is to keep you from getting through and who is probably too busy to do much talking anyway.

Of course, you should be *prepared* to talk to anyone in the building. What follows, then, is a brief summary of the predilections of the people in the four major categories within your organization, as well as some ideas for topics you should find out more about in any dealings you may have with that person.

Consumers

These people focus on *functions.*. If your company were introducing the world's first color photocopier, the Consumer would probably be most interested in *how* to use this new device. Would it need special paper, for instance, that would have to be kept in supply? The consumer wants you to save him or her time, make the job easier and more fun.

When dealing with a Consumer, DO: find out what is being used now; learn how it is being used; determine whether there have been any serious problems with the current product or service; find out who's who; try to obtain non-critical tactical information for this sale only (but see below).

This bears repeating. When dealing with a Consumer, DON'T: ask a receptionist for company information—instead, ask to speak to a sales rep and direct all fact-finding questions to him or her. (Yes, sales reps are considered Consumers, and, yes, you should identify yourself as a sales rep to this person.)

Seymours

Seymours tend to focus on *features.* The feature of your color photocopier might be that it copies thirty documents per second. As you know, I suggest you try to avoid Seymours on the first call, but when you do finally call on them after your meeting with VITO, here are some general guidelines to follow.

When dealing with a Seymour, DO: take everything he or she says with a grain of salt; try to find out the technical criteria of the product or service; focus on "how much/how big/how long" kinds of specifics; ask what else Seymour has been looking at and what Seymour likes about it; ask what the perfect solution to the problem in question would be if Seymour designed it. (You'd better get comfortable before you ask this; the answer may take some time.)

When dealing with a Seymour, DON'T: ask, "What's next?", "Who's making the decision on this?", or "What's the procedure followed here in setting up this product (or service)?" (Instead, do *tell* Seymour what should happen next.) Also, *DON'T* ask Seymour whether the organization is happy with the current product or service. The answer you get is always yes, regardless of the facts of the situation.

Managers

These people focus on *advantages.* The advantage of your color copier will be tailored to many unique departmental needs. Managers must deliver winning performance by staying ahead of schedule and under budget.

When dealing with a Manager, DO: establish the person's perception of current departmental needs; ask about current and future projects and priorities; find out how long the organization has used the current source of supply, and whether that source is meeting the department's needs. (Note: Unlike Seymour, the Manager may be a good source of reliable information on the decision making process within the company.)

When dealing with a Manager, DON'T: ask about likes and dislikes with regard to the current product or service. If this manager recommended the current source, you may well hear only about the likes. Instead, ask, "Is the current (product or service) still serving your needs?"

VITOs

VITOs focus on *benefits* and little if anything else! The *benefit* of that color copier could be that it will enable VITO's sales staff to assemble proposals that will attract more customers.

VITO wants to know how your solution will help the company realize its fullest potential, and, without anything even vaguely resembling hedging, what bottom-line results can be expected.

What follows is a *brief* summary of some of the most important factors to keep in mind during your first conversation with a VITO. (*Note:* The topic of your all-important first call to VITO is covered in much greater detail later in this book.)

When dealing with a VITO, DO: ask about specific goals; ask about VITO's criteria for establishing a business relationship; confidently ask what it will take for VITO to do business with you. (And wouldn't VITOs love their own sales reps to ask that question of each and every prospect!)

When dealing with a VITO, DON'T try to do "company research" by quizzing VITO about the organization's history of using your product or service or a competitor's product or service. VITO may not know!

■   ■   ■

To close this chapter, I want to refresh your memory with this re-vised outline of the Influence and Authority Network, which shows you where each of the four categories stands in relation to the other, and reviews some of the key questions you should be prepared to ask.

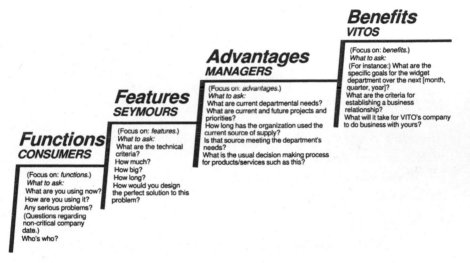

A Little More on Benefits

The concept of the benefit is so important to understanding the world in which VITO lives that I want to review it very closely with you before we move ahead in the book. (Some of what follows was already dis-cussed briefly at the end of chapter five, but it's important enough to look at once again.)

Parinello's Definition of a Generic "Benefit"

- A desired result.

- A measurable improvement over existing conditions.
- Added value (getting more than you paid for).
- A gain in a desired direction.
- A return on investment that exceeds expectations.
- Progress that leads to new opportunities.

Parinello's Translation of Tangible Benefits ("Hard Dollars") into VITO's Desired Results

Following are examples of *tangible results* VITO could realize from your solutions.

- Increased efficiency
- Measurable increase in revenues.
- Increased sales.
- Greater market share.
- Substantial decrease in fixed or variable expenses.
- Reduced time to market.
- Reduced cost of sales.

Parinello's Translation of "Intangible Benefits" ("Soft Dollars") into VITO's Desired Results

These intangible benefits usually align well with the benefits of doing business with suppliers.

- Reduced risk and worry.
- Greater convenience; ease in completing daily tasks.
- Ability to set new trends.
- Ability to be the first to recognize a new marketplace.
- Recognition; praise; esteem by industry, peers, or community.
- Increased customer loyalty.
- Improved employee morale and motivation; improved labor relations.

■   ■   ■

So much for the call objectives. In our next chapter, we'll look at some additional methods for getting information about VITO's organization.

Chapter Eight:
More Research You'll Need to Do Before Contacting VITO by Mail

At some point before you make your first contact with VITO, you may decide it's appropriate to go beyond phone research on that new company. Such research may help you prepare yourself for your later letters and calls, and it may play a major role in the customized letter you'll be drafting in the next chapter.

By the same token, many salespeople (and I'm one of them) find that you really don't need a heck of a lot of company research to prospect VITOs effectively. What you really need to know about is the profile of your *current* customer base—and then you need to know, in very broad terms, whether the VITO you're calling, fits the same major categories. My experience is that, if I know that 85% of my current customers operate widget-processing firms employing between 50 and 100 people, with headquarters within an hour of downtown Los Angeles, I can find out through calls to company sales reps whether or not I'm well advised to write a letter. If VITO's firm seems likely to fall into the target category, I write the letter. If it doesn't, I don't. I don't worry about whether VITO has worked with products like mine before, or under what conditions, or what the results were. A good portion of the time, *VITO* doesn't know about any of that stuff. (VITO tends to see things first in terms of his own organization—not in terms of the vendors that organization hires.) I figure that, if I know how I'm helping my current customers, and I know that VITO *could* fit their profile, I know enough.

You may decide that more research is in order, however, and in your circumstances that may make perfect sense. So here are some other ideas for tracking down information about VITO's company.

Call and Ask Someone at the Front Desk or in Investor Relations to Send You a Brochure, Catalog, or Annual Report

Cheap, easy, and static-free—and infinitely preferable to trying to earn ten minutes of the receptionist's time with "a few quick questions." When combined with an upbeat call to one of the company's sales reps, this approach should get you a wealth of information.

Buy a Share of Stock in VITO's Company

I'm not kidding. If the firm is public, and if you're really gung-ho about tracking down good, solid company data, call up Investor Relations (or a broker), ante up the money, and take a look at the information the shareholders are getting. Obviously, this is a technique best employed when you have a little time. It may be perfect for that plum account you've had your eye on over the last year and a half, but can't quite crack.

Cruise the Information Superhighway

There are a number of efficient ways to use on-line information services to track down important information about companies. For my money, however, a trip to the library works just as well, but in the end it's your call and your time.

One of the metaphors I like to use in describing the way you must deal with VITO is this: *You are not trying to close a sale; you are applying for a job.* That job, partner to VITO, is a tough one to land.

Now, if you were preparing for a real-life job interview at a particularly highly ranked firm, one at which you knew many other top-notch applicants were also interviewing, you might well decide that it was worthwhile to boot up your computer—or make a few phone calls—and engage in a little electronic digging. For a particularly important spot, why not try to do a little on-line research if it will help you to shine at the interview?

If you decide that such an inquiry is in order in researching VITO's organization, you may want to use the article search features available on such services as CompuServe, Prodigy, or even the Info-Track service available at some of the larger libraries these days. Alternatively, you may wish to contact a service such as Nexis Express, which can search its immense databases for earning and finance reports, stock records, and much more—and get everything to you in short order. Check your telephone directory for contact information for these electronic resources.

All of these services require some sort of fee. If you're new to the idea of searching for data on-line, you may wish to recruit a friend who's well versed in the search methods of each service to track things down for you. Wandering aimlessly around cyberspace for four or five hours in search of the perfect bit of data can be an extremely expensive way to impress VITO!

CHAPTER NINE:
BENEFITS—AND THE
HEADLINE OF YOUR LETTER

Finally! You're ready to start working on your letter to VITO. Its first and most important component will be a headline statement.

Let me warn you once again that this is going to be a letter unlike any you have ever written. It will be only one page long, with the other side blank, but it will probably require more care, patience, and consistent effort than any other piece of business correspondence you've ever written. Since you'll be spending some time developing a couple of drafts of this letter, we'll deal with the actual content of the message first. Then we'll look at the physical form your letter must take. Note that this aspect, too, will be quite unlike your other written communications to prospects.

The letter we'll be crafting in this part of the book is for *VITOs you have not yet contacted.* After a little bit of practice, you'll be able to adapt the formats to other VITOs, as well.

How This All Started
Now, let me give you a little background on how I came up with the idea for the letter I use to reach VITO. A few years back, I started to look closely at the letters salespeople were writing to their prospects. I tracked down actual letters from actual salespeople, and I looked at the advice all the business-letter books were offering on how to compose correspondence to prospects. And by that I mean I went to the library and looked at every book on the topic, and went to the bookstore and *bought* every book on the topic that I hadn't seen. After looking at all that, I was horrified. The only saving grace I could find in the letters I looked at was that they were, in virtually all cases, going unread by their intended recipients.

One of the books that I read on how to write a good business letter was written in the year I was born—1947—and do you know what? The basic outlines of what that book suggested are still being parroted in today's books!

Do you think the average decisionmaker today has just as much· time to read correspondence as the average decisionmaker had in 1947? Well, neither did I. The format you're about to see is a creative, original approach that I came up with after reviewing the needs and time pressures of *today's* reader.

The very first person I sent my new-format letter to was the president of a big high-tech firm. (I'd also been sending out a number of other letters to top people, letters that pretty much followed the standard formats.) Three days after I put it in the mailbox, my phone rang. I picked it up and said, "Hi, this is Tony. How can I help you?" A voice on the other end of the line said, "You sent my president a letter. He circled two words and gave it to me."

I said, "Oh? Which two words were those?"

The voice said, "The words were 'satisfaction guaranteed.' That's got to be a pretty big business risk for you, huh?"

"Actually," I replied, "it's one of the lowest business risks I've ever taken. Out of the twenty thousand people I've worked with, *nobody* has ever been dissatisfied. By the way, who is this?"

It was the executive vice president of sales and marketing of Texas Instruments.

With that kind of result from a single letter, I had a feeling I was on to something. Experience has borne out that I was right. If you're half as excited now as I was after getting that first call, you'll be in a great position to take advantage of the letter we're about to review.

A word of advice before we begin: *Follow the instructions in this chapter to the letter.* By doing so and following up by phone as outlined later in the book, you will be taking advantage of a technique that has, for me, yielded an *85 percent* contact rate with top decision makers. Yes, you read right: 85 percent! Considering that the most common reason we hesitate to contact VITOs directly is their supposed inaccessibility, don't you think it's worthwhile to give this method an honest try, without altering it in any way?

The Headline Statement

Research shows that, on average, people decide within about eight seconds whether or not to continue reading an unexpected piece of mail. VITOs, of course, are not average, and some of them are likely to make that decision a little earlier. Therefore, you must earn VITO's attention within the first eight seconds, tops, and probably a few seconds earlier than that. You're going to need a compelling Headline Statement to do this job.

You'll place the statement at the top of the letter. When you read a newspaper, what's the first thing *you* look for? Headlines! VITOs, of course, read newspapers every day—so use the same principle here. Put your most compelling material at the top of the page. *Don't* include any superfluous, textbook, business-letter material—such as VITO's company name and address—in that all-important spot. VITOs already know where they go each morning and what the name of their company is. Make the Headline Statement the first thing that anyone seeing this letter would notice.

With this statement, you must win interest and avoid pre-judging. In its most powerful form your headline:

- is no more than 30 words long.
- addresses this VITO's interests and is relevant to this VITO's industry.
- establishes your credibility.
- references a specific time frame.
- establishes your Equal Business Stature. (Remember, you are not approaching VITO as a salesperson, but as a businessperson.)
- is based on a *literal quotation*—or on verifiable *factual information*—from a credible source your VITO will recognize and respect. Typically, this source is either another VITO in the same or a similar industry or a recognized publication such as a trade magazine or industry newsletter. Another excellent source would be a quote from a VITO who sits on the Board of Directors of the company you're trying to do business with. Or, if your company is currently doing business with a retail firm, and if your product, service, or solution can also be used by a

bank, you could make a very powerful appeal to the VITO who holds the top position at a bank by repeating the high praise for your company given to you by one of the bank's best customers! (How do you find out what bank your retail customer uses? Take a look at the next check they send you!)

- highlights or is based on the tangible benefits of doing business with your company.

- highlights or is based on the benefits of doing business with your company. (Please take a moment now to review the tangible and intangible results VITO desires from his partners. You'll find the summary in an earlier chapter.)

Your Headline Statement should sound the trumpet for actual events, not hypothetical situations. By this I mean that you should focus on measurable results that real, live customers have enjoyed from implementing your solutions—results that feature percentages or other figures and *always* incorporate a specific time reference.

Words to the wise: VITOs hate generalities! They have learned from bitter experience *not* to trust phrases like "in the near future," "on or about," "approximately," or any similar language with built-in wiggle room. Far better to do a little research (believe me, your Headline Statement is worth it) and offer phrases like "in sixty days," "two weeks ahead of schedule," and "sixteen percent under budget."

Your Headline Statement *may* include your company name, as long as it comes *after* the name of a customer's company. (As you'll see a little later when we talk about stationery, the idea here is not to broadcast your company's name or logo, but to isolate solutions to VITO's problems.) Your Headline Statement *may* include words like *guarantee, discover, benefit, value, advantage, proven, results, quality, progress, growth, safe,* and *genuine*—but if you have a compelling third-party endorsement that omits these words, there's nothing wrong with going with that.

Wow!

That's a lot of requirements for a thirty-word statement! I'll be honest with you, it's quite possible that it will take you a good deal of time to find or craft just the right Headline Statement. But your letter is worth it.

Let's say you're selling laptop computers. Here's an example of how your Headline Statement might evolve:

```
High-resolution screen would be easy for your
salespeople to read.
```

to:

```
Salespeople can file reports quickly and
accurately
```

to

```
Salespeople can spend more time with customers
```

to:

```
Our work with salespeople has shown that they
are consistently able to spend more time with
their customers.
```

to:

```
Our work with our customers indicates that
salespeople can increase the time they spend in
front of their customers by as much as 50% —within
two months of using our laptops.
```

to:

```
Our work with our customers indicates that
salespeople can increase the time they spend in
front of their customers by as much as 50%—within
two months of using our laptops—without
increasing the cost of sales.
```

to:

    We've increased the time XYZ Company's
salespeople spend in front of their customers by
30%-50% in just two months and maintained the cost
of sales.

                    ■   ■   ■

Yes—you can, if you wish, completely eliminate any reference to your
product or service. In fact, it may be an advantage for you to do so!
Remember, your goal is to build interest and keep VITO reading.

    Take a few minutes now, on a separate sheet of paper, to write a
rough draft of a compelling Headline Statement. Try to come up with
one that would stop VITOs in their tracks and keep them reading, even
though they have fifteen other important things to do in the next hour.

Headline Statement

_____

_____

_____

_____

_____

_____

_____

_____

_____

_____

_____

_____

_____

_____

_____

_____

_____

_____

Have you completed a draft of your letter's Headline Statement? If not, please stop here and do so.

If you have decided to use a direct quote from a respected source as your Headline Statement, but have not yet located the quote you want to use, you should *draft the quote* and submit it for approval. That's right—many times when I ask VITOs for a quote, they'll ask *me* to come up with wording for *them* to approve.

Here are some Headline Statements that work. How do yours compare?

(Audience: Mammoth Auto Company parts suppliers and engine suppliers.)

Mammoth Auto Company plans to reduce its suppliers by 50% in the coming year. We can show how you can use this to *increase* your revenues from Mammoth, starting today.

Note the inclusion of the Mammoth name as the very first elements of the statement, a tactic guaranteed to win the interest of a VITO whose company sells to Mammoth. Also good here is the use of the term "revenues" rather than, say, "profits"—a term, by the way, you should *never* use in this letter or in any other communication with a VITO.

What if VITO's goal for the company this year is to lose one million dollars instead of twenty million, as it lost last year? What if, as is commonly the case, the Accounting Department takes its sweet time telling VITO whether or not there *are* any "profits"? Why remind VITO of that? (I'll tell you a secret—some VITOs have no idea how the company's "profits" are computed in the first place!) All raising this issue will do is get VITO mad in those first eight seconds, and you don't want anger. You want attention.

Of course, as powerful as that Headline Statement is, it would be even more so if you could incorporate a quote from Mammoth's annual report specifying the change in plans. Talk about credibility!

(Audience: the dean of Marywood College.)

We've lowered Armstrong College's student registration operating costs by 30% in less than six months. Armstrong was also better able to deal with the new state reporting regulations.

Some nice things here, not the least of which is the specific record of delivering a measurable result (30% lower operating costs) within a definite period of time (six months). If you've made it this far in the book, however, you should already know that, if you have the slightest doubt about your company's record with regard to these results, *don't tell VITO you've done it!* VITO will very likely call up the president of Armstrong and ask how that student registration system is running. Tell the truth and be accountable.

Now, you're not promising (yet) that you can deliver the same results for VITO. You are reporting what, exactly, you've been able to deliver to other VITOs.

Note the use of "we" in the opening sentence of the last Headline Statement. That's a very strong formulation; it gets VITO wondering who's talking, and it's infinitely preferable to its two alternatives: your company name, or the word "I." The company name is to be avoided because it can encourage prejudgement on VITO's part. Use of "I" with a VITO is problematic if your objective is to build rapport. "I" is too self-centered; it takes the focus off VITO's favorite person (VITO) and puts it on someone about whom no information is available (you). VITO doesn't yet have any reason to care about you as an individual! You as a team member, however, may well have some solutions to offer. Stick with "we."

■   ■   ■

(Audience: president of a large California public television station.)

We helped KXET in Santa Monica maintain solid customer service and reduce delays in premium deliveries to donors—while reducing operating costs in Donor Services by 34%.

That unprepossessing "while" is important; it means you're paying attention to both ends of the equation, just as VITO has to. Did you miss it? Look again. This Headline Statement tells VITO that you have been able to reduce delays *while* lowering operating costs.

Think about it. VITO hasn't gotten to the top spot by assuming that it's *impossible* to lower expenditures and increase quality or efficiency at the same time. Quite the contrary! VITO usually makes a habit of *assuming* there must be a better, cheaper, *and* faster way to do the same job his organization is doing now—if only his people would find that way!

Be one of those people. Find examples of how your company has helped your customers raise revenues *without increasing payroll expenses*. Tell VITO about the time you helped a customer get a product to market early *without compromising quality*. Locating such solutions is what real businesspeople in the real world have to do every day. Don't just promise to lower VITO's costs. VITO doesn't need your help for that—all that's necessary is a quick trip to personnel and an order to send a hundred pink slips out! Or nix an ad campaign! Or cancel a company party! On the other hand, lowering VITO's costs *while increasing output*—that's worth listening to.

Work both sides of the equation. When you do, you'll demonstrate to VITO that you can really tackle the tough problems. VITO's problems.

■ ■ ■

(Audience: the senior partner of a major law firm.)

```
We've reduced overhead costs in five of the
top ten law firms in Dallas—and, according to
Helen Wells of Wells & Wells, "increased billable
hours by 25% in the last 90 days."
```

Look how much is gained by the use of that quote! VITO almost *has* to pay attention. But note that the person quoted is not a direct competitor of VITO's—or, at least, is not likely to be. You've quoted (with permission, of course) a senior partner from an out-of-state firm. (If your VITO worked in Texas, you'd find another headline.) Avoid directly quoting or citing competitors in your Headline Statement; it may be perceived as threatening. If you feel it's appropriate to cite your performance with someone who's competing with VITO, use the formulation that appears in this Headline Statement: "five of the top ten widget firms in Yourtown." That delivers important information but keeps things in the abstract. Of course, when asked by VITO to give details, you will.

■　　■　　■

(Audience: president of a large consumer goods corporation.)

"Jones and Company views XYZ as a strategic partner, crucial to the success of our business. XYZ will help keep us positioned as a leader in the retail clothing industry."

> Andrew Jones, President
> Jones and Company
> 1994 Annual Report

Certainly nice if you can get it. Now, I grant you, your firm may not be the subject of glowing paragraphs in the annual reports of your customers—but are you sure there are no other forums in which the results you've delivered have been trumpeted to the skies? More to the point, have you ever *asked* your current customers to describe the work you've done for them? Let me repeat this. You may find that your customers are so happy with what that they've been getting from you that they won't mind if you draft the endorsement yourself for their approval! If you find yourself in this enviable situation (and my guess is that, with very little effort, you can), take the time to find *exactly* what your company has delivered—then draft a hard-hitting Headline Statement *that you then take to VITO for approval*. It bears repeating: You must be a straight shooter here. Not only is it the best and only way to build the reputation you want, but to indulge in the alternative—composing and circulating quotes that your contacts haven't seen—is to limit your own career growth and court catastrophe for your company. VITO is just the type to call to check on these things, and it isn't going to do your cause any favors if the person you quote mumbles something about having met you once a few months ago and not remembering much else.

Don't cut corners. When developing endorsements, get all the proper authorizations. (Of course, that front-page *New York Times* article calling your company the single most dominant player in your industry can be quoted in your letter without further ado.)

The example given above doesn't cite specific figures. It works, but I'm going to encourage you to try to track down actual performance numbers from your customers anyway as part of the development of your Headline Statement.

Many salespeople, when asked to work with customers to develop specific figures and time references like those included in many of the previous Headline Statements, start to get cold feet. "Tony," they say, "I don't know the exact [employee turnover percentage, increase in billable hours, reduced time to market, or whatever] at this company, and neither does my contact. I can't get bogged down with this kind of stuff!" If this is your reaction, read the next few paragraphs very carefully, because we've just touched on something of paramount importance—something that will affect not only your Headline Statement, but your whole campaign to sell to VITO.

You cannot sell to VITO if you cannot produce documentable successes.

No ifs, no ands, no buts, no maybes. If you are unwilling to do the research necessary to find out exactly what kind of results your product or service has delivered for your customers, you should stop reading this book right now, because it's not going to do you any good. *VITO needs proven benefits,* and success stories preceding them. If you can't deliver same, don't bother trying to work with VITO.

Feeling unenthusiastic about tracking down the numbers? Well, get enthusiastic! Find out what you're actually delivering to your current customers. (And note that the much-maligned, analytical Seymour may be your most valuable ally in this effort.) What would happen if you got a call on Monday morning from the VITO at you your prize account? "This is VITO—I want you to get your fanny in here and justify your existence. The budget ax has fallen, and we have to cut half of our vendors. Be in my office at two o'clock."

How's that for motivation? Well, guess what. That's the call you're lucky to get! The most common case is the one in which you simply fade away from your customer's list of preferred suppliers and partners. No comment, thanks. Goodbye.

Rationalizations for Not Doing the Research

Now, people come up with all kinds of reasons not to do this step. "The organization is too complex." "The products are too far removed from the end users." "Spreading these figures around—if we ever determined them—would be a breach of confidentiality because our competitors might hear about it." "Our customers buy so they can fill out their budgets at the end of the year." Then there's the most popular one: "My customers won't give it to me." My response: baloney! If you ask, they will give you the information.

You provide benefits to your customers—to VITO. If you want to be able to survive in today's marketplace, you must be able to show VITO exactly why and how and how much and how soon there will be a benefit to VITO's organization. Then—and this is more important than anything—you must keep VITO *conscious of the value of the relationship with you at all times.*

This is not to say that you must necessarily incorporate hard facts and figures into your Headline Statement. A compelling quote from a satisfied customer that doesn't discuss specific performance data can also work wonders. (The quote from Jones and Company's annual report would be an example of this.) But you must *at some point* be willing to provide measurable details of the success stories you've made possible for your customers—and, just to be on the safe side, you should be able to recite chapter and verse on such success stories within, oh, say, a few seconds of encountering any VITO. Don't worry, we'll be covering this in full a little later in the book.

Now, then. This "I-can't-be-bothered-with-tracking-that-down" reaction that I get from salespeople sometimes arises from an (understandable) uneasiness at the idea of trying something new. That's human. We all tend to fear the unknown, and what I am telling you to do here is not common behavior for most salespeople. For the vast majority of us, the sale is either closed or pending; the customer is either happy or unhappy with what we're doing. The idea of *initiating* contact with a customer, and then trying to find out exactly *how* the product or service is performing, in terms that a VITO will understand and give credence to, is foreign. As foreign as it may seem, though, it's something you will have to give an honest try if you're going to see results from this part of my program.

If your initial skepticism about what I'm suggesting is rooted in a feeling that you've simply never *done* anything like this before, congratulations. Assuming you've got happy customers somewhere, you've got it easy. All you need to do is work through the preconceptions you may have about "what a salesperson does." Ask for a meeting with a contact at your best account. Ask how what you've been working on has affected operations there. Ask for estimates of specific performance levels over specific periods of time. Ask for permission to incorporate these estimates into your sales materials, and provide all necessary confirming materials so your contact can approve what you'll be circulating.

Once you track down and quantify your product or service benefit, you will improve your rapport with your current customers, and you *will* see success from this program by incorporating the new information into your presentation to VITO. I've seen it happen too many times to think otherwise.

If, on the other hand, your hesitation comes from a well-founded suspicion that there may not *be* any success stories to speak of in your customer base, or a fear that if you were to call most of your current customers to go over the details of your product or service, they might act to cancel the account when reminded that they're doing business with you, then you've got big problems.

■　　■　　■

(Audience: CEO of a firm experiencing market share problems.)

"Excellent! I would highly recommend this seminar to all my colleagues—but not to my competition."

> Bill Wyerson, Sales Rep
> ABC Company
> Corvallis, Oregon

This one demonstrates that a compelling Headline Statement can be considerably less than thirty words long—good news for VITO, because he doesn't have time, patience or inclination to wade through a single extraneous word. (Please remember, too, that even a statement that is thirty words in length or shorter can be wordy, repetitive, and uninteresting.)

If you are inclined to work out an arrangement with one of your contacts to adapt this specific Headline Statement to your line of business, feel free to do so. That goes for anything in this book, of course, but I mention this quote now because it is concise, to the point, and extremely powerful. It's likely to serve salespeople in any number of industries quite well: "Excellent! I would highly recommend AAA Widgets to all my colleagues—but not to my competitors."

Just remember not to send a letter using this opening to any of your contact's competitors! Doing so would be a breach of trust, of course, but even if your contact for some reason didn't mind such use, it wouldn't earn you any points with the VITO reading the letter.

■   ■   ■

(Audience: Owner of a small chain of Arizona hotels.)

"Green Roof Inns has increased its revenue by 9% and improved customer service and satisfaction during the past year since implementing XYZ's guest communication services."

David Dawson, Owner
Green Roof Inns
of Connecticut

Here's someone VITO can trust, someone VITO knows looks at the world as a businessperson. Here's a fellow VITO.

If you can secure a quote like this one, a quote from a *noncompetitive* fellow VITO who is familiar with or active in your VITO's identical line of work—or a similar line of work—use it. (A good bet: a quote from a VITO active in the same industry as your VITO, but in a different component of that industry. You might use a quote from a well-known literary agent, for instance, in a letter to a VITO who is the president of a publishing company.)

Words to Consider Using in Your Headline Statement

Good
Money
Easy
Guaranteed
Health
New
Proven
Results
Safe
Save
Own
Best
Complimentary

Try Again

We've spent a lot of time reviewing the Headline Statement, and there's a reason for that. It's probably the most important part of your letter. If the Headline Statement works, you will have gained VITO's attention. (And, by the way, that's the only goal here—to win attention and draw VITO into your letter. You are *not* trying to convince VITO to purchase your product, service, or solution.) If your Headline Statement doesn't work, your letter goes into the circular file with all the other ignored messages of the day.

So: Now that you've had a chance to review a number of Headline Statements that work, why not take this opportunity to rewrite your own? Revising and reworking your efforts is a critical part of this process. If you have only completed one or two drafts of your statement, odds are very good that it is not yet ready to include in your letter.

Please take the time now to revise your Headline Statement. Then proceed with the next chapter.

CHAPTER TEN:
THE REST OF THE LETTER TO VITO

Assuming that you have succeeded in crafting a powerful Headline Statement, it's now time to move on to another part of the letter. But it's probably not the part you're thinking of!

In a standard letter, after establishing the "grabber," the opening lines on the page, most of us would be inclined to move on to composing the body text. But we're going to focus on the elements of this letter in their order of importance—which means that we'll be looking at things in the same order that VITO does. (Actually, this is the order *anyone* in VITO's organization would read the letter, including VITO's secretary or assistant, who will probably be reading this first.)

Now, we know VITO is a very busy person, and we can make a guess, based on that, that this very busy person is not likely to read each line without satisfying a natural curiosity about who's making such dramatic and expressive claims. (Indeed, one of the main purposes of your Headline Statement is to instill curiosity in the reader.) So the next most important part of the letter will not be the body text, but the part of the message appearing at the *very bottom of the page*. In other words, we are going to take advantage of VITO's next move, which is going to be to leap from that headline statement down to the signature line to find out who on earth has sent this letter.

There, beneath your signature, VITO is going to find—and read—a very prominent Action P.S.

Unlike the Headline Statement, the Action P.S. follows a very definite form. It won't take you twelve drafts to develop. It may, however, require a little more telephone work—about which we'll talk in a moment.

The Action P.S. should look like this:

P.S. I'll call your office at 8:00 am on Thursday, January 23. If you will not be in, or if I've chosen an inconvenient time, please have Tommie tell me when I should return the call.

Tommie, of course, is VITO's secretary or assistant. If you don't have VITO's secretary's name, you can't write the Action P.S. Believe me, replacing what appears above with "have *your secretary* tell me when I should return the call" will not work! So don't try that.

Remember, this is a customized letter. You must specify the secretary's name because *he or she is the person who will almost certainly be reading this letter first and deciding its fate!*

When Tommie opens the envelope and reads that P.S., what do you think is going to happen? Your letter survives, that's what happens! Tommie will be mightily impressed that there is someone out there who knows that he or she plays a vitally important role in making things happen for VITO. Tommie will probably check VITO's calendar and write in your calling date. Tommie will almost certainly be expecting your call. Tommie may even call *you* to say something like, "Ms. VITO will be out of town on the 23rd—but if you prefer, you can give her a call at 8:00 on the morning of the 24th." (Don't laugh—it's happened to me hundreds of times.)

But what if you don't know the name of VITO's secretary? That's easy. Presumably, you have already got VITO's name—otherwise there's really no point in drafting the letter. (You may want to review the ideas on finding company information that appeared earlier in the book. My first course of action is always to consult the business directories, such as the *Million Dollar Directory* or the *Corporate Yellow Pages*, at the local library.) To find out the name of VITO's secretary or personal assistant, call the company's reception desk and ask something along the lines of, "Does Ms. VITO Benefito spell her last name with one or two Fs?" You'll get an instant answer and no conflict whatsoever. Then say, "Thanks. By the way, what's her secretary's name?" You'll have exactly what you need.

Don't Skip That Call!

I should say here that the "how-do-you-spell-that" call technique I've just outlined is good to follow even if you happen to know the name of VITO's secretary. There are two reasons for this. First of all, it's a good idea to doublecheck everything going out on paper to VITO, and the spelling of VITO's name is certainly no exception. Secondly, you should be dead-certain in your *pronunciation* of VITO's name as well as its spelling.

I once contacted a VITO whose company was located in Florida. The directory I consulted in the library told me that the president's name was Guy Rabat. I don't know how you'd pronounce such a name if you came across it in a directory, but to me it registered as "Guy Rabbit." "What an odd name," I thought to myself. I had to do my normal routine of checking the secretary's name—and checking, for that matter, that Mr. Rabat was still the president of this firm, and that I was spelling and pronouncing his name correctly. (I have learned from bitter experience never to give directories the last word on names and titles. They are, to some degree or another, out of date from the moment they hit the bookshelves. Often, they are flat-out wrong to begin with.)

So I called the receptionist and asked, "Could you tell me, please, does Mr. Guy Rabbit spell his name with one or two 't's?" She laughed out loud and said, "It's not 'Guy Rabbit,' it's 'Guee Ruh-BAH.' There's only one 't', and it's silent because he's French!"

Can you imagine what would have happened if I hadn't taken the time to call to make sure of the spelling and pronunciation of that name? If I'd written the letter without doublechecking, and followed up by calling and asking to speak to Mr. Rabbit, the president? If the receptionist had chuckled to herself, thought, "Here's a dumbbell who deserves whatever he gets," and put me through?

"Good morning, Mr. Rabbit. How are you today?"

That's what I call a "reload." You shoot yourself in the foot once, open the chamber, reload, and shoot yourself in the other foot. Don't do it. Check everything before you send out the letter.

■   ■   ■

Once again, *use the exact format I have described here for your Ac-*

tion P.S. Don't play around with this. The wording here is important, and what I've provided really does work.

A note on scheduling the time of your calls to VITO is in order here. The approach that works for me and for the many salespeople I've trained is to set aside a whole day, schedule each call to a VITO every half hour, and focus on initial contacts for the entire day. I strongly suggest you follow this method.

Verticalize your letters. What do I mean by that? I mean you shouldn't pretend that the same letter that works for a senior partner at a law firm will work for the president of a manufacturing firm. Your letters must be industry-specific, heavy on experience and research, and compelling for the intended audience. That means you must address your letter to the concerns of a top person *in that industry*, and customize wherever you can. (To take the opposite, or horizontal, approach is to assume that all VITOs are concerned with the same issues, which is manifestly not the case.)

Warning!

Do not send VITO any letter with an Action P.S. attached unless you are *positive* you can follow up with a call at the time you indicate!

Actually, you should probably count on calling approximately two to three minutes *earlier* than you indicate in the letter. (Being early, by the way, is always what VITO means by "on time.") Woe unto you if you promise VITO that you will call Tuesday morning at 8:00 and the phone doesn't ring until 8:12! (And if you hold off until Wednesday, of course, you can simply forget about doing business with VITO.)

Remember—VITO lives in a world that cries out for *tangible results.* Your claim to be able to provide these will very likely be irreparably undermined if your first call to VITO is not a punctual and professional one.

Susan, a salesperson who took my seminar recently, had an unfortunate experience. She planned to send out a single letter as a test of the system. (Not a fair test, but never mind.) Her letter went out to the VITO at the largest health maintenance organization in the eleven western states.

The next Friday afternoon, as Susan is closing out one week and getting ready for the next, the phone in her office rings. It's VITO's secretary. (That's a very common outcome, by the way, and a great start to your sales cycle.) The secretary says, "Susan, I see here that you're planning to call VITO at 9:00 on Monday morning. VITO's asked me to have you call him at 7:30 because he's got a staff meeting at 9:00. Here's his private number—use it so you can bypass the switchboard, which won't be taking calls until 8:30." Talk about a golden opportunity!

Unfortunately, Susan stayed out a little late on Sunday night with some friends who asked her whether or not she'd ever drunk tequila before. She hadn't, and to this day, I'll bet she wishes she could still say that. On Monday morning, she *woke up* at 7:30, scrambled for her notes, did her best to coax something resembling her normal voice out of her throat, and punched VITO's number. She was not ready for the call. And she blew it.

First of all, she ended up calling five minutes late, which is a near catastrophe when dealing with VITO. Worse, she was trying to speak to him from a blank spot within a yellow haze that hung like a puffy halo around her head. That's another example of a reload.

You can't do that with VITO.

Don't let it happen to you. Be ready to roll and in top form when dealing with VITO—and do whatever it takes to keep your promises. If you are faced with a sudden emergency, find someone to make the call for you.

Here's a Real Letter

The rest of the elements you'll be putting together for the letter will be easier to understand if you take a look at the genuine article first. Please bear in mind that the letter that follows is not something to *copy*—your experience, your industry, and your prospects will determine the actual text you use. But in terms of the structure of the letter, this will serve as a good model.

Important note: The format of your final letter should use an italicized larger font for the Headline Statement. The body of the letter should be set in a crisp, professional-looking font.

"Sickland Regional Medical Center has increased its earnings by five percent in the past four months. They achieved this by using the American Care Association's sponsored program with XYZ."

Dr. John Cuttersmith
Director, SRMC

December 14, 1994

Ms. Vita Benefito
President

Dear Ms. Benefito:

Sickland Regional Medical Center will have an additional $257,000 this year to pay for its new pediatrics wing. This is money they would have spent unnecessarily on administrative expense had they not discovered our unique business solutions.

Here are some of the major benefits that Massachusetts medical centers are realizing as a result of selecting XYZ as a strategic business partner.

- 20-30% increased accuracy in claims.

- Shorter reimbursement cycles from insurance carriers—by as much as 60 days.

- 5-10% decreased bad debt.

Can your medical center achieve similar results? Frankly, right now it's hard to tell. But one fact is certain. You are the one person who can take action to find out. Together we can quickly discover exactly what the possibilities are.

Sincerely yours,

Will Prosper
XYZ
555-1321

P.S.: I will call your office on Monday, May 21 at 9:30 a.m. If you will not be in, please leave word with Tommie as to when I should return the call.

You probably recognized the Headline Statement and the Action P.S. at the top and bottom of the page. Now let's look in detail at the rest of the letter, the components that make up the body of the text.

The Tie-In Paragraph

This is what comes immediately after "Dear Ms. Benefito." Write a *brief* opening paragraph that follows the theme of your headline and will tie in to the benefits you're about to list. This part of the letter has to take the headline, follow the theme it has established, and bring the reader to the body of the letter. Although there are very few words here, this is a critical component of your letter.

Here are some examples of the kinds of tie-in paragraphs you should use.

■　　■　　■

XYZ company has helped hundreds of local companies turn (category) cost into an effective business tool, rather than a business expense. We do this in the following ways:

■　　■　　■

During the past several years, we have worked with many companies in the (VITO's industry) field, including (names of those companies). Together we've been able to reduce costs, increase efficiency, and provide a competitive edge in the following ways:

■　　■　　■

There has never been a better opportunity for companies like (name of company) to demand more from your (source of supply). To satisfy your needs, we must give you the competitive edge to distinguish you from your competitors! Here's how we've done it for other firms in your industry:

■　　■　　■

Now, if you've written introductory letters to prospects before, this approach may come as something of a shock. But let me be plain: I want you to completely eliminate any opening pleasantries, any small talk, any mention of discussions with the receptionist at VITO's company—in short, anything and everything that doesn't relate to a benefit for VITO.

"But Tony! Shouldn't I follow standard business format, with VITO's address at the top of the page? The sales books I've read tell me that I should take a few sentences to develop rapport! My sales manager tells me to follow the examples in the sales books!" Now, I know full well that *most* sales letters open with a little chitchat. And I know that *most* sales letters follow the "rules" set down in sales books and other manuals. But most sales letters don't get results. Yours will. (Show your sales manager this part of the book if that helps your cause.)

How many letters do you imagine VITO receives that open with a textbook-perfect date, address, and salutation, and then continue with something like "I just wanted to introduce myself . . ." or "As a result of a discussion with Mike, your receptionist, I wanted to suggest that we might . . ." or "Ms. VITO, have you ever wondered how top performers . . ." or "Hi, my name is . . ." or anything else of the kind? How many? Dozens! Hundreds! Thousands, maybe! Honestly, now: What do you imagine happens to those letters?

Those openings (and their many companions) are guaranteed blind alleys with failure rates so high that salespeople have talked themselves into believing that a five-percent (or three-percent or two-percent) contact rate after sending them is somehow satisfactory. Well, it's not. As I mentioned earlier, you can do a heck of a lot better—specifically, you can reach VITO during your follow up call in the neighborhood of *85 percent of the time*. So stay away from the familiar, comfortable openings.

The Bullet Text: Nothing But Benefits

No features. Just benefits! That's the body of this letter. You must offer *only* short, meaningful, results-oriented statements that compel VITO to read every word. By that I mean a series of bullets (typically, three to five of them) that concisely state your best business benefits in order of importance.

You must identify credible, hard-hitting benefits of your solutions. Remember that benefits are both tangible and intangible.

The benefits you outline must relate to VITO's interests and be clearly connected to VITO's industry. They should not require explanation or elaborate technical language; in fact, technical terminology, industry buzzwords, product numbers and the like should be avoided entirely in this letter. The benefits you select must be customized to your business and to VITO's needs, and so I strongly advise you against trying to copy the examples that follow word-for-word. However, these benefit bullets will give you an idea of the style and form yours should take.

■　■　■

(Our consulting firm has helped clients:)

- Retain or increase market share in 85% of all cases.
- Shorten the launch window for new products by an average of one full month
- Decrease initial quality complaints from consumers by an average of 24% within two months.

■　■　■

(Here are some of the benefits area businesses are realizing as a result of selecting XYZ as a business partner.)

- An average of 13% increased quarterly revenues.
- Reduced production expense—with time savings ranging from one to six months and no compromises on quality.
- In the words of Jack Miller, president of ABC Enterprises, "an overwhelming increase in the efficiency and positive attitude of our support staff."

103

■　　■　　■

(Our seminars have helped participants:)

- Obtain greater market share by creating more new business with prospects—in some cases, 70% more!

- Increase customer retention and eliminate erosion of hard-earned market share.

- Use their sales time more efficiently, so that they spend an average of 40% more time in front of likely customers.

The Body Copy: The Closing Paragraph

Next, we move to the closing paragraph. You may be tempted here to suggest a date and time for an in-person meeting. Or to suggest that VITO would be the perfect candidate to benefit from your product or service. Or to give VITO your 800 number to call for more information. Or to tell VITO that you look forward to doing business together. Don't do any of that.

Let me repeat: The material you develop for your letter, and specifically for your opening and closing statements, *is not intended to sell.* As a matter of fact, one of my favorite approaches in the closing paragraph is to express a measure of objective skepticism on the question of whether or not the results I've been able to deliver to others will be able to be repeated at VITO's company. Can't you just see it? VITO reads that and starts stomping around the office, thinking, "Why *not?* Why *can't* you deliver these results to my company?"

After all, you're not like all those other salespeople who tell VITO how wonderful what they have to offer is before bothering to learn a thing about VITO's business. You're different. You're a businessperson who's eager to find mutual solutions, and you know that VITO hasn't had any input on what you have to offer yet. So you're going to stay detached, removed, and professional. you're going to focus on *VITO's* reactions, judgments, and opinions—not yours.

Here are some examples of closing paragraphs that work.

■   ■   ■

Could your company realize the same substantial benefits? Frankly, I'm not sure. But I would welcome the opportunity to learn more about your unique business needs and take the first steps to find out.

■   ■   ■

Could your company receive equal or greater benefits from our solution? We're prepared to help you determine the answer.

■   ■   ■

Does this sound like something your company could benefit from? We could find out what the possibilities are in only (20) minutes. Looking forward to sharing profitable ideas.

■   ■   ■

Would you like to find out if your company can achieve similar (savings and efficiencies)?

■   ■   ■

Would you like to explore the ways (XYZ) will be able to meet your specific business needs?

■   ■   ■

We would like your valued opinion on some of our growth management solutions and how they might work for you in (year).

The Body Copy: An Overview
Naturally, you'll have to spend some time making sure these three

pieces—opening, benefit bullets, and closing paragraph—fit together properly. Here are some examples of strong body copy that does the job.

Note that your name, company, and phone number appear beneath your name and signature. Your phone number must appear here—otherwise interested VITOs or their associates will not know how to reach you if they want to reschedule the time at which you will call. (By the way, this happens quite a bit.)

Here is another example of body copy—in other words, the letter minus the Headline Statement and the Action P.S.—for you to review. Please remember that the "right" letter for you to send to *your* prospects is the one that *you* develop—not my letter.

(Audience: president of a medium-sized publishing house.)

December 14, 1994

Mr. VITO Benefito
President

Dear Mr. Benefito:

Our electronic inventory system took order-turnaround time from an average of three days to an average of twenty-four hours within three months of implementation at twelve of this state's twenty largest-volume publishers. Here are some of the major benefits that these publishers are realizing as a result of selecting XYZ Systems as a business partner.

- 10-20% lower overall return rates.
- More orders from large accounts. (In some cases, 25% more.)
- Faster and more accurate in-store setup on high-profile title launches.

XYZ is making it easier for publishers like you to achieve similar or greater benefits. Together, we could find out what the possibilities are.

Sincerely yours,
Will Prosper
XYZ
555-1322

That's less than 150 words, but they're words that count. They're VITO's words.

Putting It All Together

Now we've taken a look at all the text elements of the letter. Here's a template that will help you remember the way everything falls together on the page.

**"Grabber" Headline Statement, taking the form
of either a quote from a fellow VITO or a
compelling statement of quantifiable success.
Should not exceed thirty words.**

Date

Mr. VITO Benefito
President

Dear Mr. Benefito:

Opening two (or, if brief, three) sentences that
follow the theme of your headline. Focus on actual
savings, increased output, or increased efficiency at
real-life companies. Finish the story begun in the
headline. Then continue with . . .

- Your very best business benefit.

- Your next best business benefit.

- Your next best business benefit.

One good way to close the letter is to leave open
the question of whether or not the results you've
outlined can be duplicated at VITO's company. Leave the
ball in VITO's court and suggest that, together, you
and VITO can work to determine whether or not the
partnership you're suggesting will be likely to work
out.

Sincerely yours,

(Your signature)

Your name
Your company name
 and phone number
(NOTE: YOU MUST WITHOUT
FAIL INCLUDE YOUR PHONE
NUMBER HERE!)

P.S. Say here that you will call VITO's office at
such-and-such a time on such-and-such a date. If VITO
will not be in, or if this is a bad time, ask that VITO
have (name of VITO's secretary) to advise you of a more
convenient time.

Now, that's not your standard business letter, I'll admit. But you know what? It works.

VITO *Can* Tell a Book by Its Cover

It's time to talk a little about the physical form of your letter.

VITO is called on to make dozens of important decisions daily. When it comes to issues VITO (or VITO's secretary, for that matter) considers to be less than earth-shattering, such as whether or not to read letters from new business contacts, *appearance counts*. Put more bluntly, if VITO *can* save a step by stereotyping your letter ("I know what this is; they're trying to sell me something") and ignoring your message, VITO will—usually within seconds.

If you send that letter, on which you have spent so much time isolating issues of specific interest to VITO, and make it look identical to your ordinary business correspondence, you aren't stacking the odds in your favor. As a matter of fact, you're practically begging for someone in VITO's organization to toss that letter out. Even if it does reach VITO's desk, you're still sending a *unique* message in a *deadly dull* format that, for VITO, might as well be a neon sign: "Like All the Others." Don't undercut that carefully crafted message. Don't undo all the work you've done. Make this letter look different.

You must assemble this letter in such a way that it includes little or no external or internal material identifying it as sales-related. This is not because you want to deceive anyone, but rather because you are following through on your commitment to project an image that is different from that of most salespeople. As a group, of course, salespeople are generally oblivious to VITO's real concerns. Accordingly, you won't be sending out letters that look like theirs.

Here are some of the most important guidelines for getting your letter opened—and routed all the way to an attentive VITO.

Don't Use a Standard Letter-Sized Envelope

They get lost in the shuffle too easily, because they look like everything else that comes over the pike. Use a large catalog-sized envelope, and place that unfolded single-page letter in it without paper clips, brochures, articles, or any other distracting materials.

Don't Use Envelopes or Stationery Bearing Your Company Logo

Instead, use plain white stationery and a plain white envelope.

I get a lot of static from sales managers on this one, but the results are worth whatever trouble you may have to go to in order to get this issue to come out your way. The question is not one of "projecting your company image," or "demonstrating quality and commitment to customers," or "standardizing everything that goes out of the office," or anything else that your company logo is supposed to do. The issue, instead, is *keeping this letter alive.* Logos cause preconceptions, and preconceptions cause people to "prioritize" correspondence. We don't want this letter prioritized (that is to say, put in a pile; that is to say, ignored). We want whoever sees this letter to conclude that there is no alternative but to pass it along the chain to VITO.

Let's say your company designs engineering software systems and is called Lightning Technologies. If VITO or anyone in VITO's organization sees "Lightning Technology Services, Inc." at the top of the letter, any one of the following thoughts may overpower your message.

- "We already have computers."
- "We don't handle weather forecasting products."
- "We already have software."
- "We don't need consultants."
- "This is junk mail."

Your company's logo may be beautiful. It may have cost tens of thousands of dollars, and an army of consultants may have been required to develop it and place it properly on the company stationery. But on this letter, in this setting, with this objective, it *cannot* appear. Your initial correspondence with VITO must be free of any, repeat any, distraction from that painstakingly crafted message.

If people in your organization are adamant on the stationery issue (and a good many sales managers are), do what I do. Put together 50 letters according to the instructions that follow. Then put together 50 letters that are set up as the sales manager would do it. Then follow up by phone as outlined in the next chapter and see what happens. The non-stationery approach always wins. Always.

Don't Use Address Labels

You have written a customized message, not one piece from a scattershot mailing. Your letter must look the part. Type the address on the envelope, or write it out by hand (if and only if you have attractive handwriting).

Don't Use Metered Postage

Stick regular *first class* postage stamps, preferably the peel-and-apply variety that's now available. (Did you know that each standard postage stamp you lick contains *eleven calories?* And believe me, you don't want to know what they make that glue from.) You're going for a personalized approach, so don't deviate from this. Bulk rate postage screams "sales message"; overnight delivery services may be effective, but they're awfully expensive considering that you'll be contacting dozens and dozens of VITOs. Express services are really your call; you may decide that using, say, two-day priority mail makes sense for particularly important VITOs.

Do Use A Return Address on the Envelope

But don't mention your company. Instead, use your name and the company address.

Don't Put Anything Else on the Envelope

Specifically, don't use trick phrases like "Personal and Confidential," "To Be Opened by Addressee Only," or any of the other cute phrases meant to keep people from opening VITO's mail as they've been instructed to do. We *know* someone besides VITO is going to open VITO's mail. (What's more, we know that these "privacy" techniques are likely to lose us points with VITO, who doesn't have time for games.)

Customize, Customize, Customize

Because you're reading a book rather than taking a seminar, I can't give you close personal mentoring here. You'll have to do work to develop a letter that will work within your industry. I want to emphasize here, though, that with the significant exception of the Action P.S., *everything* appearing in the letter to VITO must be customized to your unique selling environment. Work up a letter that's compelling because of what you know about your industry. Fine tune your letters to each of your solutions and each of the potential vertical markets within a given industrial category. Once again, *do not* try to send a letter that's "just like" the ones that appear here. They won't work for you.

Three True Stories

True Story Number One. I once followed up on a letter to a VITO in Florida by calling, as promised, at 8:30 a.m. Florida time. My office is in California, so that means I had to make the call at the crack of dawn! I reached VITO's secretary, who told me, "VITO is on the shop floor right now, but he's expecting your call. Let me have him paged for you." I waited a moment. VITO picked up the phone, but made no mention of the fact that I was calling at 5:30 California time. (VITOs run on a time zone of their own—VITO Standard Time—and everyone else is off schedule.) No, what I heard from the other end of the line was VITO asking me, "How do I know you're as good as you say you are?" I was delighted to tell him the success stories that demonstrated the point.

True Story Number Two. Luanne, a salesperson who worked for a very conservative investment firm, was dubious about drafting and sending the letter I've outlined in this chapter. She was afraid she'd get resistance from "the people upstairs." "If you do," I said, "just say this. You're trying a new program—one they paid for, by the way—that says it delivers an 85-percent (or better) contact rate with top decision makers. You can't follow the program without sending the letter. Suggest a sample mailing of 50 letters, and then follow the rest of the program to see what happens."

A few weeks later, Luanne called to tell me she had done as I had advised, and had gotten the reluctant approval of "the people upstairs." "How are things going?" I asked. "Great," she answered. "I ended up talking to forty-three of the fifty people I targeted—and I have appointments with five VITOs this week." I said, "Ah, that's wonderful, Luanne. Listen, just out of curiosity, how many VITOs had you been able to set up appointments with before trying this technique?" "Well, Tony," she said, "I've been here for two and a half years, and by the end of this week, I'll be up to, uh, five."

True Story Number Three. Brian, a St. Louis sales rep, took my seminar and had a question about the Action P.S. He said, "Tony, I have to call nine VITOs at major local power companies, and I want to send all the letters out at the same time. What do I do about the time I mention in the P.S.?" I said, "Block out half-hour slots, assign each slot to one VITO, and just make the calls." He did—and he got through to seven of the nine VITOs. (It was a heck of a morning.) One of those seven contacts resulted in a $1.25 million sale, on which Brian received a $48,000 commission. That sale was finalized within three months of the day Brian sent out his letters—and this in an industry in which the average sales cycle is one and a half to three years!

What Now?

You've developed a compelling, customized letter for VITO that is likely not only to reach its destination, but to arouse interest in what you have to offer. Now what do you do? In the next chapter, we'll look at the specifics of your initial telephone contact with VITO.

Chapter Eleven:
Getting VITO's
Attention by Phone

In this part of the book, we'll be examining the phone techniques you should use to follow up on the letter to VITO we discussed in the previous chapter. You should know that the ideas you'll find outlined here can be applied *whether or not* you have sent the letter we examined in the previous chapters. Because the call is most powerful when it follows a letter, my preferred method of dealing with VITOs who have not yet heard about what I have to offer is to send the letter first and call as promised. For VITOs who fall into other categories, you may decide to call first.

What I'm about to show you can be used whether or not you send a letter first. It can stand alone. (Note well, however, that during the call you will be using much of the research and endorsement material you use in developing the letter, so you shouldn't try to skip those important steps.)

Not Just Any Call

Just as you took a little extra time and effort to research your letter to VITO, you must work a little harder to prepare for your phone follow-up than you would if you were contacting another person in the prospect's organization. Believe me, you don't want to let 7:55 roll around, pick up the phone, punch VITO's number, hear a voice say "VITO here," and proceed to use the standard opening statement all those sales books out there point you toward. VITO has heard it all before—and will quickly conclude that that sharp letter you sent along was nothing more than an aberration.

No, your call will be different. Three to five days after you are reasonably certain VITO's office received your mail, you will, as promised and on schedule, initiate contact with VITO. *If you are serious about building a business partnership with this VITO,* you must be prepared for a rapport-building encounter between two professionals of Equal Business Stature. *If you are serious about building a partnership with this VITO,* you will be prepared for the first step on a journey with VITO's organization—a journey that begins the minute you make telephone contact with *anyone* in VITO's office—and will, if you are successful, have no end.

Let me be clear on one point. When I talk about establishing Equal Business Stature with VITO, I don't mean that you should try to mislead VITO into thinking that you are more successful than you are, and I certainly don't mean that you should exaggerate your organization's record of accomplishment. I mean you should present yourself as the knowledgeable professional you are! I mean you should take the leap from quota-chasing salesperson to businessperson! You are an understander of—and solver of—VITO's unique problems.

At this point in my seminar, there's usually a hand raised to ask a question: "Tony, what happens if I don't get through to VITO when I call at the time I mentioned in the letter?" Well, if you've done your job correctly up to this point, the odds are pretty good that VITO will be expecting your call. But, truth be told, not all your calls will result in direct contact with VITO that first time.

What if you get shut out by others within VITO's organization? In the chapter that follows this one, we'll examine the best way to handle calls that result in contact with VITO's secretary and seem to stop there. I say "seem to" because far, far too many salespeople view being "stuck" talking to VITO's secretary as the end of the road. It's not, and once I outline the simple (but amazingly effective) technique for dealing with the personal assistants and secretaries who work for VITOs, you'll understand why! But more on that, and on the sometimes trickier question of dealing with people at reception desks and switchboard consoles, a little later. For now, we're going to examine what you should do when your first call does make it through to a VITO who is ready, or at least willing, to take your call. And trust me, if you send out enough well-researched, well-constructed letters like the ones we looked at in the last chapter, you're going to run into quite a few VITOs who'll take your call the first time.

Making Your Opening Statement Stand Out

You may be used to saying something like this when you call decision makers:

> "Hello, Mr. VITO, this is Will Perish calling you this morning from XYZ Associates. How are you today? Great. Hey, did you receive that letter I sent out to you on the twenty-third? Oh, well, it must have gotten lost. Listen, I'll tell you the reason for my call; we handle the world's largest widget accounts here, and I believe that in a brief twenty-minute meeting, I could show you some of the competitive advantages. Is Tuesday morning or Wednesday afternoon best for you?"

And so on. As familiar as you may be with that phone script or some variation of it, I want you to do yourself a favor and forget you ever used it. Toss it out the window, because it simply won't cut any ice with VITO. Once you develop your Ultimate Opening Statement, you'll be able to use a compelling, attention-grabbing statement that will remove the burden of "making" VITO do anything (which is impossible, anyway).

Here and now, we're going to break the conventional telephone habits that flash red "salesperson alert" lights at the VITOs of the world and make them disconnect from you. We'll hone and polish your current phone skills and develop the Ultimate Opening Statement—the opener that is your very best bet for winning interest and attention from a VITO.

The Ultimate Opening Statement: Definition and Goals

The Opening Statement is *not the entire conversation.*

It is not meant to sell VITO anything, or persuade VITO of anything, or convince VITO to meet with you.

It is what you say *until the other person begins to speak.* Period.

It must encourage VITO to interrupt you. You read right: that's the primary goal of the first fifteen to twenty seconds of your call. The secondary goal is to sound conversational. The opening statement must be delivered in a cordial, natural, and unthreatening business tone. It must be said with conviction, passion, and enthusiasm—but it must not seem frenzied. Keep things relaxed, even if VITO doesn't. That means you will have to practice the statement we develop in this chapter until it sounds spontaneous and professional throughout. If it sounds canned, as though you're reading from a script, you lose. VITO will tune you out. If it sounds confrontational or abrupt, you lose. VITO will perceive you as someone who will waste precious time.

There's a fine line to walk here. Cordiality does not mean you abdicate any responsibility for participating in the conversation; being conversational does not mean that you are entitled to leap ahead to levels of intimacy with VITO that you have not earned.

Get interrupted. Keep the tone cordial. That's everything as far as the main goals of the Opening Statement are concerned. So you can forget about image-making, conveying important information, distinguishing yourself from your competition, and anything else you may be tempted to insert into this part of the call.

As a matter of fact, before we start crafting exactly what you're going to say, we should examine these goals in a little more detail—as well as what your Opening Statement must *not* do under any circumstances.

The Opening Statement Must Avoid, at All Costs, Pushing the Two Fear Buttons

The statement you use must *not* trigger the two greatest fears VITOs have about talking to salespeople. The first is that we'll waste their precious time, a legitimate concern that I think is pretty self-explanatory. The second is that we'll talk about something that they themselves are ill-informed about (and, not infrequently, couldn't care less about). When we do this, we challenge VITO's power, control, and authority, and that's something to avoid at all costs.

When we ask VITO something like, "VITO, have you considered the many advantages of a computerized de-fragmentation system for your document storage and retrieval pathways?", then attempt to close by asking something obnoxious like, "Is Monday at two or Tuesday at ten best for you?", guess what? We push *both* of these fear buttons. (That appointment-choice method, as you may know, is known as an "alternative close." Avoid it like the plague.)

When we say things like this, we sound exactly like salespeople—

and VITOs know from bitter experience that the single best way to punch a hole in a busy schedule is to spend half an hour or so on the phone with salespeople who know nothing about the problems piling up on their desks. And in all likelihood, VITO neither knows nor cares about the possibilities of computerized de-fragmentaion systems for document storage and retrieval pathways!

How's that for a shocker? VITO has no idea about the pros or cons of the features you have to offer. VITO *doesn't have time for details*. VITO hires people who *do* know and care about such things as computerized de-fragmentation systems—namely, Seymours. To ask VITOs whether they have "considered" these things is to highlight nuts-and-bolts areas of the business about which VITOs generally know little or nothing. That's not the way to build business rapport!

The Opening Statement Must Permit VITO to Retain Power, Control, and Authority

Remember, your goals are to *get VITO to interrupt you* and to *keep the tone conversational at all times*.

To permit VITO to retain power, control, and authority, you must keep the focus on VITO's favorite person—VITO—and away from you. Of course, you will not, for any reason, interrupt VITO. But there's a lot more to the authority issue than that.

For one thing, you will never, never, never use the word "I" in your Opening Statement. And, just as in your Headline Statement, you will *not* begin by introducing yourself with "Hi, my name is (name), and I work for . . . " or anything like it.

Forget about VITO for a moment. When *you* get a call that begins with, "Hi, my name is . . . .", aren't *you* tempted to tune it out immediately? Now imagine you have an organization to run and a big staff meeting coming up in five minutes. How much time and attention are you going to give the call?

Let me be honest with you about what I'm proposing here. It's quite difficult. We're all human, and humans tend to focus on "I" first and others second. *Eliminating the instinct to open with some form of "I" takes practice!*

It's common practice for us to begin a call with "I'd like a few moments of your time," "I was just wondering," "I'd like to introduce myself," "I just wanted to know if you'd be interested in . . . .", "I'd like to tell you about," or any of a thousand other "I, me, mine" formulations. But you can't do it with VITO. I've said it before, but it bears repeating here: *VITO doesn't care about you.* So do whatever it takes to keep yourself from falling into the habit of opening with an "I" statement.

In addition, letting VITO maintain control means that you have to fight another salesperson's instinct: asking for an appointment. In your Opening Statement, you will use your time to provide solid business reasons for VITO to tell *you* to come in for an appointment. VITOs *like* to tell people what to do. That's what they do all day long! Fine, then. You're going to let them!

People may tell you to ignore my advice about avoiding the alternative close. After all, dozens of sales training books tell you to ask VITO a question like, "Would Monday afternoon at four be a good time for us to meet, or would Tuesday morning at eight be better?" Is this really the kind of question you ask someone who enjoys telling people what to do? Of course not. But VITO hears it again and again. Offer a change of pace. Don't say anything of the kind. By the end of the conversation, VITO will have either decided not to work with you, told you to come in for an appointment, or pointed you toward someone else in the organization. (The first outcome is going to happen now and again, and if you've had any time as a salesperson that won't come as a huge shock to you; the second and third outcomes, of course, each represent a golden opportunity.)

Letting VITO maintain control means that you won't ask stupid questions like, "You *are* interested in raising revenues, *aren't you?*" You must never try to force a "yes" out of a VITO, or back VITO into a corner, or hold VITO hostage to an earlier remark.

The Opening Statement Must Help You Transmit an Unforgettable First Impression

You'll do this by focusing on *measurable benefits*, just as your letter did. In doing so, you'll distinguish yourself from the vast majority of VITO's business contacts.

You must come across as a seasoned, experienced professional who will stand by the results of the program offered—no matter what.

The Opening Statement Must Be Tightly Focused on Getting VITO
to Want to Find Out More

This call is your only person-to-person opportunity to convince
VITO of the importance of meeting with you. That means you have no
time to get sidetracked. Accordingly, you will *not* mention your benefit
letter or ask if VITO has read it.

That's right. You are not going to reference your letter! You're going
to avoid doing that at all costs. Think back. In your own experience,
haven't you had the experience of saying to someone, "Hey, did you get
my letter?" and having them reply, almost automatically, "No, I didn't."
And where do you go from there?

If you ask VITO "Hey, did you get my letter?", you're really only
doing one of two things. You're either challenging VITO by suggesting
indirectly that the letter was never opened in the first place, or you're
implying that VITO has a memory so poor that it can't retain a simple
thing like having read a letter. Neither of these are particularly good
places to start a business relationship.

By the way, I strongly advise against asking VITO *any* "yes-or-no"
questions that sound even vaguely like closing maneuvers at this stage.

> *You:* "VITO, have you considered signing on with this kind of
> program before?"
>
> *VITO:* "No. And I don't think I will now."

Why run the risk of exchanges like this? VITO is in charge, not
you. Tossing off "yes-or-no" questions at this point makes the exchange
a little too close to that of a prosecutor and a hostile witness. ("Now,
VITO. Did you or did you not agree that you would consider using our
widget service during our last meeting?") You don't want on-off responses from VITO. You want broad visions of what the future holds.
You want VITO to do what VITO does best—expound on opinions, company goals, and objectives!

Because you will take every precaution against allowing VITO to
get sidetracked, you will *not* discuss the ease or difficulty of getting
through to VITO. And you will *not* appeal to any internal "referral" by
saying something like, "Tommie said this would be a good time to

reach you." You will stand on your own two feet, highlight your record of delivering solutions, then get VITO's valuable opinion and direction. Period.

Always Remember: The Opening Statement Must Encourage VITO to Interrupt

Never forget that the primary goal of your Opening Statement is to get VITO to interrupt you. After all, the person who is speaking has power and control over the situation, and there should be no doubt in your mind now about who that person is when it comes to your interactions with VITO.

You will build in pauses to your Opening Statement, pauses that allow VITO to talk while you listen—and I do mean *listen*—to what is said. When VITO interrupts you, *you win,* no matter what is said. (Hard to believe, I know, but it's true.)

VITOs are lousy listeners. Yes, you read right. I'd estimate that, on their best days, they are less than completely attentive to what others have to say about eighty percent of the time. Managers get paid to listen to their valuable team members; Seymours *live* to listen, to compare, to contrast, to analyze. As you move up in the Network of Influence and Authority, you find that listening skills get worse and worse . . . and VITO, the worst listener of them all, is at the top of the heap. We're not going to fight that fact by asking an obvious question (such as "Are you interested in increasing your sales?") in a misguided attempt to stop VITO cold and force a "yes" answer. We're going to use the fact that VITO is a poor listener to our advantage.

(A side note: you may think that my observations on the listening habits of top decision makers are exaggerated. A recent study by Madelyn Burley-Allen, the nation's leading expert on listening, validates that VITOs are the very worst listeners in organizations.)

So—what *do* you say when VITO answers the phone?

Item One: The Sweetest Words in the English Language

The first words out of your mouth after you hear "VITO here" will be the most important words in VITO's life. Any guesses?

You've got it. VITO's name.

- "Mr. Benefito."

or

- "Ms. Benefito"

This usually break's VITO's preoccupation with whatever crisis has just descended on the office, and probably wins you a second or two of interest. Use formal address ("Mr. Benefito" rather than "the first name") until you are invited to do otherwise.

Practice the Opening Statement we'll develop in this chapter until it becomes second nature to you. (And don't practice on VITOs. You'll lose appointments, sales, and business relationships.)

Item Two: The Pleasantry

Do *not* follow your natural instinct to supply your own name after mentioning VITO's. In fact, you will not, at this stage of the Opening Statement, offer any introductory material of any kind. Instead, you'll use a sentence that introduces some kind of pleasantry. I like to say something like, "Mr. Benefito, it's great to finally speak with you."

Here are some more examples of pleasantries that work.

- "Thanks for picking up the phone."
- "It's a pleasure to speak with you."
- "Your time is important, so let's get right to the point."

Don't ask "How are you today?" or any variation thereof! The ritual of asking our conversational partners this is part of our social conditioning, and the instinct to do so on the phone is extremely strong. Nevertheless, when dealing with VITO, we must reprogram ourselves, because engaging in this habit in this setting is a guaranteed way to turn off VITOs. You disagree? Well, what runs through *your* mind when a total stranger asks you something like "How are you doing today?" Do you stop whatever you're doing to be sure you don't miss a single exciting minute of the conversation that follows?

Sometimes, when I get a call from a salesperson who obviously knows nothing about me or my organization, who is obviously making a cold call, who butchers my last name because calling ahead to confirm the pronunciation is too difficult, and who asks "How are you to-day, Mr. Parionellio?"—sometimes, when I get a call like that, you know what I'll say? "Grab a big piece of paper, this is going to take us a few minutes. I'll tell you how I am. Okay. Now, we just got two little kittens, and we thought we had them trained to use the litter box, but as I got out of bed this morning, guess what I stepped into? I didn't really realize what it was until I took several steps across my antique Persian rug. As if that weren't enough, after I took my shower I went to use my electric razor, and darned if it hadn't broken. Just would not switch on. So that put me even further behind schedule this morning. Later I went outside to start my car, but the battery was dead. My wife had left the vanity mirror on. Anyway, this is the kind of morning I've had. So I'm glad you're calling to ask how I am today. Did you get all that?"

That's brutal, I admit. But to my way of thinking it's just as brutal to ask a completely insincere (and unconstructive!) question like "How are you today?"

You get the idea. Stay away from your (often intense) instinct to ask VITO "How are you?" Use a pleasantry that sounds sincere: one that doesn't ask a question you don't really want to spend time explor-ing, and that lets VITO know you mean business.

Item Three: The Conversational Bridge

After your pleasantry (and, again, bearing in mind that you *want* VITO to interrupt you with a question or comment), you will be ready to use a conversational bridge that will lead you to your first benefit statement. The bridge will sound something like this: "During a conversation with Jane McLaughlin at Cambridge Light last week . . ."

Here are some more examples of conversational bridges that work.

- "While visiting Acme Corporation last week . . ."
- "As we speak, Acme Corporation is enjoying . . ."
- "Together with Acme Corporation, we discovered . . . "
- "Mark Houghton over at Acme Corporation said . . ."
- "Salespeople at Rogers International have found . . ."

You should be ready to employ short bridges to get from any one phase of the dialogue to any other phase. However, you must not use the bridge to cut VITO off or to change the subject on an issue of importance. Remember, VITO must feel in control.

Item Four: The Hook

Your hook is a *verbal rendition of the Headline Statement in your letter*. However, you should never deliver it verbatim as it appeared in the letter. The Headline Statement is the written word; your Opening Statement is the spoken word. *Each requires a different formulation.* You could say something very vague in your Opening Statement, letting the listener draw conclusions and put pieces together. You can't afford to do that in your written headline! What we want VITO to think is, "Gee, this sounds familiar." We *don't* want VITO to think, "Here's someone who's got something memorized—there's probably a canned speech coming in about ten seconds." (And when you take as your objective that of reminding VITO of your Headline Statement, rather than repeating it, you'll actually hear things like, "Didn't I read about this in the newspaper?")

Here are some examples of hooks that work.

- "Jane told me she'd been able to reduce four major elements of ABC's overhead costs by 24% as a result of using our solution during the first quarter."

- "Acme Department Stores realized a $12,000 monthly reduction in retail unit costs. That money helped subsidize a new ad campaign—which in turn boosted their third-quarter earnings!"

- "Acme Construction decreased down time by 12% in the first three months using our solutions."

Keep the exchange conversational, but, in the absence of any direction from VITO, keep it moving toward this hook. The sooner you repeat the benefit VITO read about in the Headline Statement of your letter, the sooner you are likely to be interrupted with something along the lines of, "This sounds familiar. Did you send me a letter?"

Important! When VITO says that or anything similar to it, whether at this point or at any other, *stop progressing through this Opening Statement* and say, "Yes. What did you think of it?" Then *let VITO talk—while you take notes!*

If VITO does not interrupt you in this way, pause and continue with . . .

Item Five: The Introductory Phrase

This is the point at which you tell VITO who you are and who you work for. The phrasing is important here. As you are no doubt well aware by now, using "I" or "my name is" won't get you very far. Instead, say, "Mr. Benefito, Will Prosper with XYZ."

Of course, if VITO asks your name at any point in the conversation before this, you will supply it. The advantage of waiting to *offer* your name and affiliation until this point is that VITO may be more interested in knowing who you are once you repeat the benefit you outlined in your headline letter.

Item Six: The Ending Question

This is where you ask about VITO's specific business interests, or whether VITO feels your solution might be worth exploring further. *Do not ask for an appointment. Do not ask for a purchase decision. Do not ask an obvious question in an attempt to force VITO to say the word "yes."*

Your ending question should incorporate the element of time ("this month," "this quarter," "this year"). This is very important. One basic way to ask this question would be to say, "VITO, are you looking for a new way to help you lower your cost of sales?" The better way to ask it would be to say, "VITO, are you looking for a new way to help you lower your cost of sales *by the end of next month*?" Do you see the difference? Now try to balance it out by integrating the other side of the equation. "VITO, are you looking for a new way to help you lower your cost of sales *without reducing customer loyalty* by the end of this month?"

And, of course, you should aim at getting VITO to speak while you listen closely to, and take careful notes on, what is said.

The question might sound like this: "Jane's results could be tough to repeat, but would you be interested in exploring a similar program for your organization between now and the end of the first quarter?"

Here are some more ending questions that work.

- "Does this touch on issues that are of concern to you this (month, year, quarter)?"

- "Are you trying to accomplish something like this by the end of this year?"

- "Is this an issue that's important to you for this fiscal year?"

- "Is this something that's consistent with what you're trying to achieve this (month, year, quarter)?"

- "Are you interested in seeing if we could achieve the same or better results with your operation by the end of the second quarter?"

- "What would be the best way to see if we could help your company realize similar or even greater benefits this year?"

Putting It All Together

Here's a "roadmap" of what the Opening Statement will look like.

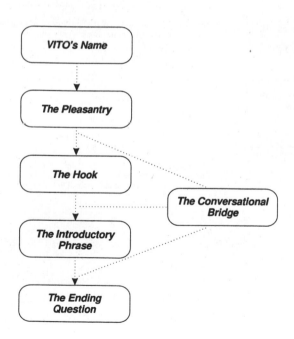

Here's an example of what a good Opening Statement should sound like. Remember, though, that your Opening Statement, like your letter to VITO, must be customized to your VITO's unique business environment.

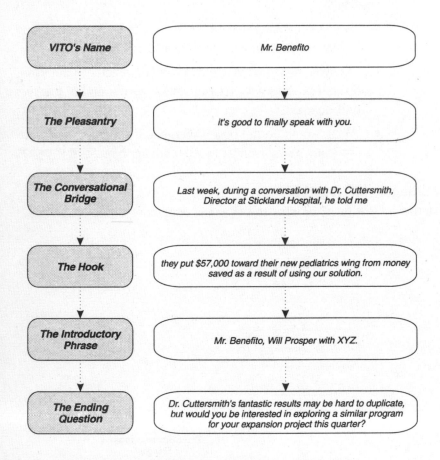

VITO's Name	Mr. Benefito
The Pleasantry	it's good to finally speak with you.
The Conversational Bridge	Last week, during a conversation with Dr. Cuttersmith, Director at Stickland Hospital, he told me
The Hook	they put $57,000 toward their new pediatrics wing from money saved as a result of using our solution.
The Introductory Phrase	Mr. Benefito, Will Prosper with XYZ.
The Ending Question	Dr. Cuttersmith's fantastic results may be hard to duplicate, but would you be interested in exploring a similar program for your expansion project this quarter?

(*Do not* ask for an appointment. *Do not* ask for a purchase decision.)

REMEMBER! Your primary objective is to get VITO to interrupt at any point during this Opening Statement! The most likely interruption will sound like this: "This sounds familiar. Did you send me a letter?"

When you hear this, you should always say, "Yes, what did you think of it?" Keep VITO talking while you *listen intently and take notes!*

Take some time now to develop your own Opening Statement before continuing with this chapter.

■   ■   ■

"That Can't Be All!"

Well, not quite. But pretty darned close.

It seems just a little too simple, doesn't it? If you feel that way, trust me, you're not alone. In fact, if you're like most of the salespeople I deal with in my seminars, you're getting a little worried about the problem of dealing with VITO's objections at this point. The fact is, though, that if you've followed the system this far, you are in an excellent position to leap over the initial objection stage and have VITO ask you—or more, accurately, tell you—when you should come by for a face-to-face meeting.

I'll tell you a secret. The objection you're probably most used to dealing with—price—is, broadly speaking, not much of an issue for VITOs. That's not to say that they don't watch pennies. They certainly do. But VITOs are looking for value, and for some new ideas that they or their staff haven't discussed yet. If they believe there's a reasonable chance you'll deliver these, they'll be willing to do the dickering later on in the process. (Or, quite possibly, have someone else do the dickering for them. That's what purchasing departments are for.)

If VITO asks you questions about potential problems with your product or service, go back to your first-call objectives. Without appearing to take control of the conversation, *ask VITO to tell you* about the following things:

- What VITO's goals and plans for the company are over a *specific timeframe.* (This month, this quarter, this year, or whatever other benchmark seems appropriate.)
- What VITO's criteria for establishing a new business relationship are.
- What it will take for VITO to do business with your company.

And if VITO *does not* pose objections at this stage, you should still ask the three questions above during your initial phone contact. (By the way, I'm not going to give you any specific order to follow in asking these questions. Just follow VITO's lead and ask the question that seems most appropriate given the direction of the conversation.)

"What's that, Tony? You mean I've got to come out and ask VITO these very pointed questions about the business on the very first call?" Yes. As a general principle, you really have to ask these three questions and your Ending Question directly and without equivocation the first time you speak to VITO. You have to ask each of them in a single sentence, without offering fifteen different options and variations. You have to ask them openly, because openness is what VITOs expect from their partners. Count on it: You'll win serious points by asking these questions directly. The courage that's required to ask them is what VITOs, deep down, expect of every salesperson in their own organization.

Yes, it takes unshakable confidence to ask these three questions. But when you do ask them, confidently and with a sense of strong purpose, you will demonstrate to VITO that you are a provider of business solutions and a reliable ally in the daily battle to attain company goals.

Don't ask VITO for everything! Focus your questions. If you ask something like, "What are your corporate objectives?", do you know what VITO will think? "Aha. Here's another lonely, behind-quota salesperson with absolutely no clue." And then VITO will say goodbye.

You must be very specific when dealing with VITOs. Ask, "What are your goals for *reducing expenses in the production department during the next quarter?*" That gives VITO something to go on.

It's worth noting here that these kinds of specific yet open-ended questions are ones VITO *loves to deal with!* You know why? Because VITO's own Managers *hate* to ask those questions! Managers know that if they ask VITO a question like that, all the decisions that were "finalized" during the last meeting will have to be tossed out the window, because VITO will have a new grand, sweeping vision for them to implement. That means new training, new software, new policies, usually without any extra money in the budget—and that means the Manager will be even more late and over budget than usual.

Well, if the Managers don't ask VITOs questions like that, nobody else in the organization is likely to, either. Do you realize what that means? That means you're the only one VITO's going to talk to all day long who'll ask the kinds of questions VITO loves to answer! So don't be intimidated. Be specific—then stand back and let VITO do the talking.

The Toughest Question

Of the questions we've outlined here, by far the most difficult for most salespeople is the one in which they have to ask VITO directly about the possibility of doing business together. Let's spend a little more time on that question now.

As long as what you come up with is direct and to the point, you can formulate this question in just about any way. Here are some examples that work.

- "Mr. Benefito, (do you have/can you think of) any potential barriers to us doing business together (this year)?"

- "Is there any obstacle that you know of to us working together on something like this?"

- "Mr. Benefito, what's it going to take for us to do this for you by the end of the third quarter?"

- "Mr. Benefito, can you see yourself as a customer of mine by the end of the first quarter of next year?"

- "Mr. Benefito, would you do business with us if we were to develop a solution in this area that worked for you?"

Are you still nervous about saying something like this to VITO? If you are, it may be because your instincts are telling you that most prospects would not react well to being asked a question along these lines. Guess what? You're right! *Most prospects* you've spoken to over the course of your working career would disengage instantly if you asked them this. But *most of your prospects have been Seymours!*

Ask Seymour this question, and, yes, you'll go down in a fireball. After all, you haven't shown any charts yet! You haven't conducted seventeen feasibilty tests! You haven't even had an in-person meeting to show off your nice color brochure and spec sheets! Seymour has no information to use in answering this question. So if you ask Seymour this, yes, you will get blown off.

But VITO is not Seymour!

If you ask *VITO* this question, odds are you'll get a straight answer.

Isn't *that* a refreshing change of pace! How many hundreds of sales calls have you set in motion with some Seymour despite the fact that neither of you knew the answer to this question? Wouldn't you rather save your time and your prospect's by addressing this issue up front? Of course you would. And so would VITO!

It may help if you think of this first phone encounter as a job interview rather than a sales call. If a job were on the line, you'd probably have a lot less difficulty saying something to VITO like, "VITO, this position is a perfect fit for both of us. What do you want me to do to nail it down?"

Well, a job *is* on the line. It's yours! You're auditioning for a job as VITO's partner. And you have to act accordingly.

When I was having such terrible trouble meeting my quota selling computer systems, I didn't have time to dance around the issue of whether VITO would do business with me. I had a target to meet and I had no time to waste. I *had* to ask VITO: "Mr. Benefito, what will it take for you to do business with us within the next six months?" And the amazing thing was, that desperate, last-chance gamble of mine really was no gamble at all! It turned out that VITOs *appreciate* being dealt with in a straightforward manner. They *respect* a salesperson who will come out and ask this question directly. This is the question VITOs want their own salespeople to ask!

If I told you you had to ask this question if you wanted to keep your current job, you'd find some way to ask it. And you'd find, as I did, that there's really nothing to fear. Let's take a look for just a moment at the reasons that may be lurking behind your trepidation at asking VITO this question.

"If VITO says no, that may block off future contact with someone else in the organization." Yes! And that's exactly the point! If you're worried about stepping on the toes of someone with whom you already have a business relationship at VITO's organization, see the later chapter on Pigeonhole Recovery.

"Maybe there's an existing vendor relationship that VITO values." Sure—maybe there is. But you're not asking VITO to give up on that vendor. This is not a closing call! If it sounds like a closing call, you're doing it wrong! This is an opening call! You're simply asking VITO *what it will take to work together.* Don't decide not to ask the question be-

cause VITO might well give you an honest answer! That's exactly what you want—and you want it now. Not months from now, when the "rubber stamp" Seymour is waiting for turns out to be not quite as routine a matter as you were led to believe.

"VITO might lie to me." Nah. VITOs are very honest. They don't have *time* to lie. It complicates things too much. They don't want to waste their own time, and they don't want you wasting the time of their key people, either. Plus, they tend to have a good deal of personal integrity. Trust me: Seymours lie a heck of a lot more than VITOs do. When VITOs tell you they see an opportunity for establishing a mutually beneficial business relationship, they mean it.

"VITO will be in a big hurry; I won't have time to fit this question into the call." True, calls with VITO tend to be very short. But take another look at that opening statement you've developed. It's lean and mean! You'll have time. When you do get in touch with a VITO, you should be prepared to go through everything you need to go through in five minutes or less. That may not seem like much time, but I'm here to tell you that, with practice, you'll find that it's more than enough.

"I don't feel that, at my level, I've earned the right to ask VITO that question." You mean you as an individual? Well, my experience has been that VITOs usually appreciate confidence and determination wherever they pop up, but for the sake of argument, let's say that you're right. You can still call VITO and ask this question. Why? You aren't making the call as an individual! You're making the call as a representative for your company! It's been in business for X years, has delivered Y results, and has paid Z dues over the years—and you're acting on its behalf. (Even if you work for a start-up firm, you're a professional offering your company's proposed solutions to a fellow professional.) Your company has earned the right—now you must take action and exercise that right.

"VITO might say no." This is the big one, isn't it? VITO might reject your suggestion outright. Despite your best efforts and confident phrasing of the questions outlined here, VITO might blow you off. Fine. You get to make your next call to another VITO. (Or, if you're a true masochist, you can call Seymour and "try to start a groundswell." Good luck.) One way or another, directly or indirectly, you're going to get the "no" from VITO. Better now than after you've spent weeks, months, or

years nurturing the account—and spending your precious time and your company's money all the while.

For my part, I do not consider VITO telling me "No, thanks" to be a rejection. Rejection, in my book, is the act of not reaching the right person when my product or service could be being used successfully—and getting cut off at the pass. Do you have to sell every single prospect in your territory to be successful? Of course not. Somebody has to say no. Don't get uptight about it. Move on. You *will* do better prospecting to VITOs than to Seymours.

There are other objections, but they all boil down to the same thing: Salespeople shy away from asking this question, but *businesspeople* don't. The first couple of times you ask it, you'll probably be a little nervous. But are you ready for a surprise? After a few times, you'll start to feel really great after making such a call to a VITO. By contrast, you'll probably agree that initial calls with Seymours tend to leave you feeling exhausted.

Warning!

Don't ask any other questions than those just outlined! Specifically, don't ask VITO to tell you "who's in charge of this" or "how purchases like these are handled." If you ask something like this, you'll be telling VITO that you're just another salesperson who knows nothing about business, nothing about the way an organization is run—and there goes your Equal Business Stature.

"VITO, I Don't Know the Answer to That, But We Have People on Staff who Do!"

"Tony, get real! VITO isn't going to let me in the door without giving me a grilling over the phone. What do I say when that happens?"

No kidding. The only way to handle this is to *state your reasons plainly, be honest when you don't know the answer, ask VITO to talk to you about one or more of the above three issues, and shut up.* And, strictly speaking, your initial call to VITO is not a success until you have either asked *all three* of these questions and received answers to them or gotten VITO to ask you in for a meeting. (In which case you will ask the three questions and more in person.)

Once again, the objective is for *VITO to do the talking and you to do the listening*. Follow the method as I have outlined it here and you will win meetings with VITOs.

Speak with confidence. Offer success stories when it's appropriate to do so. Discuss the three questions and don't ever forget that VITO's ego, power, and control are more important than yours. Let VITO drive the conversation. When you do that, VITO will want to hear more and will ask you in for a face-to-face meeting.

Words and Phrases to Use or Adapt in a Conversation with VITO

Energized
Superb
Unstoppable
Ecstatic
Excited
Fabulous
Excellent
Vibrant
Captivating
Passionate
Compelling
Perfect
Focused
Extraordinary
Brilliant
Confident
Empowered
Invincible
Driven to . .
Better than . . .
An organization like yours . . .
Discover . . .
Good
Our team . . .
Winners . . .
This month . . .

Next month's results . . .
Next month's reports . . .
Early March . . .
Early next quarter . . .
Fewer employee-hours . . .
Reduced costs in the (blank) department . . .
Plans are underway to . . .
How do you feel about . . . ?
The best part is . . .
They (other customers) surprised themselves with the results they got.
Is this something you're trying to do?
Is this something you've been thinking of?
Have you heard enough at this stage to suggest the next possible action?

Words and Phrases to Avoid in Your Conversation with VITO

I
I'm with . . .
Fear
Failure
Fearful
Frightened
Disappointed
Impatient
Anxious
Insecure
Irritated
Reject
Stress
Stupid
Overwhelmed
Overloaded
Maybe
Perhaps
Possibly
Would there be an opportunity . . . ?
Is there a possibility . . . ?
We could . . . (Instead, say: Would you like us to . . . ?)

We think . . . (This may seem safe, but it's much too close to hedging for VITO's tastes. Say what you know and can prove.)

You may be familiar with . . . (If VITO is familiar with whatever you're talking about, this is redundant. If VITO isn't, saying this will only challenge VITO's power, control, and authority.)

If you are interested . . .

(Technical jargon of any kind.)

(Bureaucrat-speak of any kind.)

Profit . . .

Profitable . . .

Are you happy with what you have? (Or any closed-ended question likely to terminate your conversation.)*

Some Additional Hints for Phone Success

So much for the mechanics of the Opening Statement. It will probably come as no surprise to you that the mental preparations you make for

---

* Please permit me a side note here on the issue of questions like "Are you happy with what you have now?" Not only should you not ask VITO this question or anything like it, you should not ask it of *anyone* at any level in VITO's organization. Sure, you may run into the occasional secretary who will give you an honest answer, but the reality is that most of your contacts, eager to move on to what they were doing before you called, will tell you the firm is *ecstatic* with what is currently in place, whether that's true or not. Furthermore, I don't believe I have ever encountered a Seymour who, when questioned in this way, would respond that there was a problem with a current vendor. If you stop to think about it, you'll probably conclude that this is your experience as well. Seymour is most likely the person who *recommended* the product. Therefore, they're not likely to say it's not doing the job.

True story: I once drove my classic 1957 Chevy pickup onto the lot of a truck dealership *with the objective of spending money on a new truck.* I was greeted by a salesperson who said, "Hey, nice truck. You've really taken care of that one, haven't you?" I thought to myself, "You know what? He's right. I really love this thing." I left the lot without buying. Six months later I drove to another dealership and was greeted by a salesperson whose first words after we exchanged pleasantries were, "Hey, how much do you pay in insurance on that?" I told him. Then he asked, "What's it like trying to track down parts for it?" I told him. Three hours later I drove a new truck off the lot. I didn't trade the first truck in; the sales rep had suggested I get a trailer hitch on the new vehicle so I could show the old Chevy off at car shows. I took him up on it.

the call will have as much of an impact on VITO as any script you assemble. Here are some suggestions on some other ways you can prepare for that all-important first phone contact with VITO.

- *Before you make your call, picture VITO's executive suite.* It's organized. It's calm. It's under control. Picture VITO dressed for success. Picture VITO calm, cool, and collected when calling an important business contact. VITO's office is usually quiet; get a good mental image of that office.

  You may not have an executive suite, but you *can* position yourself for Equal Business Stature with VITO.

- *Before calling VITO, clear your desk and put everything you need for the conversation at your fingertips.* That means your typed Opening Statement, a copy of the letter you sent to VITO, and a copy of the three questions you will ask during the conversation. You should also have ready access to a typed referral list of your best customer VITOs and their secretaries. Assuming that you have received appropriate permission, you can offer to fax this list to VITO.

  Having everything visibly ready ahead of time will boost your confidence and help make your delivery more compelling.

- *Mark points in your typed Opening Statement where you will pause briefly to give VITO the chance to interrupt you.* Never forget that this is the goal of your call. Plan to pause after every important point, name, number, or period of time.

- *Highlight important words and phrases in the Opening Statement that deserve special emphasis.* One of these should be VITO's name. Your research should help you to determine other items of interest.

- *Speak slowly, confidently, and authoritatively.* Speak at a rate that's easy for VITO to understand *and interrupt*.

- *Modulate your voice.* Vary the pitch. Keep your delivery interesting. Nothing turns VITOs off more quickly than a flat or sing-song telemarketing delivery from a salesperson. VITO has no time for amateurs, so don't sound like one.

- Ask your co-workers to cooperate and minimize background

noise. If you have to, hoist a sign that says "QUIET PLEASE—VITO CALLS IN PROGRESS."

- If possible, use a headset rather than a standard handheld receiver. This will allow you to stand up while talking (which I strongly recommend), eliminate pressure on your diaphragm, and help you to relax your voice.

- I recommend that you stand up, but if you do sit, don't slouch. Sit up straight, all the way back in your chair.

- Dress for success, no matter what else you have planned for the day. Dress as if you were meeting VITO in person.

- *Practice, practice, practice your Opening Statement*—preferably with a friend or colleague *and* by taping it and listening to it. Ask your sales manager to play the part of VITO. When your sales manager is convinced, you're ready.

CHAPTER TWELVE:
THE GATEKEEPERS

What if you can't get through to VITO on the phone?

People whose job it is to keep salespeople from reaching decision makers have been the cause of a good deal of aggravation and rejection for salespeople over the years. As it happens, though, you can use a few very simple techniques to avoid most of that aggravation. Once you review the ideas in this chapter, my bet is that you'll wonder why you spent so much time in pointless phone battles with gatekeepers.

The secret of success in this area is to remember that no encounter with a gatekeeper has to turn into a conflict. In fact, when you use the tactics in this chapter and have the right attitude, you will be able to recruit one or more gatekeepers in VITO's organization as your allies!

The Two Types of Gatekeepers

For our purposes, there are two main types of gatekeepers. The first is the receptionist or other front-line person with the job of handling not just calls for VITO, but *all* calls to VITO's organization. The second is VITO's own personal secretary or assistant. Do not confuse these two types! If you have any doubts as to the identity of VITO's personal secretary or assistant, please stop reading now and return to chapter ten of this book. You will find there a technique whereby you can verify the identity of this important member of VITO's organization.

Confusing VITO's personal secretary with a "standard" gatekeeper is a tactical mistake you must avoid *at all costs*. Vastly different approaches are in order for each!

Connecting with the Executive Suite: "Standard" Gatekeepers

"Widget Company, how may I help you?"

Let's look first at the best ways to deal with "standard" gatekeepers:

receptionists, temporary help, and other people who must deal with the switchboard at VITO's organization and field all those incoming calls from who knows how many sources.

You may be tempted to talk down to these people, but it's a big mistake to do so. Consider the following two important points.

- *Keeping track of the company's phone traffic is hard work.* If you don't think so, volunteer for switchboard duty for three or four hours at your own company. There's little time to think when things get hectic (which may be all day long). And when angry customers, salespeople like yourself, or other potentially hostile outsiders need someone to vent at, who do you think spends the most time standing in front of the fire hose? Not VITO. Not the Manager. Not Seymour. No—it's usually the first person to talk to that outsider: the switchboard operator or receptionist. All too often, the only feedback the receptionist or switchboard operator gets—even at today's supposedly "customer-sensitive" organizations—is negative. ("Why on earth didn't you tell me it was Mr. *Charles* Weenieburger? How am I supposed to know that I really should call him back if you just write "Mr. Weenieburger?") The sad fact is, receptionists are rarely if ever thanked by the companies they work for. For too many, the only time they hear the words "well done" is when someone tells them to order out for hamburgers.

- *Time is short.* Even if you were somehow able to track down a receptionist who *wanted* to engage in verbal sparring for the sole purpose of making your day go a little bit worse—which is highly unlikely—there'd be a dozen or more calls behind you blinking insistently. Receptionists really aren't out to get you—they're too busy.

All of this is by way of saying that there is simply no advantage in antagonizing switchboard and front desk people. So play it cool—don't tee off on the receptionist. Setting up grudge matches won't make your next call go any better, and it *certainly* won't win you any friends in VITO's organization. (Besides, VITO's secretary or assistant may occasionally sit in for the receptionist, so why take chances?)

Here, then, are the dos, the don'ts, and the what-ifs regarding making it past receptionists as you forge the telephone path to VITO's office. Your goal with these people is to avoid being grilled, screened, rejected, or disconnected. You're going to reach that goal by being purposeful, self-aware, and *polite* throughout the exchange. And remember, every step along the way to VITO's office can and should be a rapport-building step.

Never Ask for VITO Directly

You went to all the trouble to find out the name of VITO's secretary to put together your letter. Now, you'll use that knowledge in your call.

If you ask for VITO directly, you will be subjected to a barrage of questions designed to keep you from reaching your intended destination. "Who is calling?" "What is this regarding?" "Is this a sales call?" "Oh, VITO doesn't handle that; you want to talk to . . . " You've heard them all before. Nine times out of ten, receptionists are under orders to ask questions like this when someone asks for VITO. If you've been making calls for more than a day or two, you're already quite familiar with the typical outcome of answering these queries, and need no further instruction from me on the wisdom of avoiding them.

Instead of trying to get the receptionist to put you through to VITO, you will aim to be put through to VITO's secretary or personal assistant. You will specify this person's name. You will not volunteer your name.

Don't *ask* to be connected. Politely but firmly *tell* the person at the switchboard what needs to happen. Say, "Please connect me with Tommie in Mr. Benefito's office." Do so with confidence and a strong sense of purpose. That's not the same as being overbearing. The point bears repeating: *Do not speak in an arrogant tone of voice, as though you were about to argue with Tommie about something.* If you do, you may not be put through. Speak simply and to the point. Speak as someone who knows what is to take place next. Here it is again: "Please connect me with Tommie in Mr. Benefito's office."

Following this simple approach *exactly as I have described it* will resolve most of the problems you are probably used to encountering with receptionists and switchboard operators. Still, there are likely to be some times when your telephone partner tries to screen your call despite your best efforts to get through to Tommie. The following techniques may help you in these situations.

When Pressed, Do Not Get Flustered

If you are asked to identify yourself, or if you know that in you're part of the country it is expected that you identify yourself, *calmly and confidently* say, "This is Will Prosper with XYZ. Mr. Benefito is expecting my call at 8:30, and I'm running just a few minutes behind schedule. Please connect me." (Alternatively, you might say, "It's critical that I be on time. Please connect me.")

Never refer to your "letter." If you must say something about the reason VITO is expecting your call, read on. We'll be covering this in just a few paragraphs.

Don't Lie!

Never make it appear that you and VITO know each other. Not only is this unprofessional and not in keeping with your image as a straight-shooting provider of real-life solutions, it is extremely dangerous. You have no idea how large VITO's staff is or who talks to whom about what. And as I mentioned before, it's quite possible that VITO's assistant is *sitting in* for the receptionist. Talk about a credibility problem!

Don't cut corners. Tell the truth.

If You Are **Still** Facing Questions from the Receptionist . . .

If you follow the steps I have outlined, you will be assured of success in reaching VITO's office in the vast majority of your first calls. In the unlikely event you are *still* locked in the grip of a power-hungry receptionist, resist the temptation to turn the exchange into a conflict.

Your goal is to avoid being rejected or shunted to a lower level. You need to convince the receptionist that you have a valid business mission that's in the company's best interests.

Use a global hook that relates to the headline in your benefit letter to VITO. By "global," I mean—well, let's face it—purposefully vague. You want to give enough information for the receptionist to glean that the call is important, but not enough for him or her to be able to determine how the call should be handled. In short, you want to convince the receptionist that the person best suited to handle this call is VITO or VITO's secretary or assistant.

An example of this follows. Obviously, you will have to customize the part in parentheses to your business.

Receptionist: "What is this call in regard to?"

> *You:* "It's about giving Mr. Benefito the opportunity that my company's other customers have had to (make revenue-generating employees as efficient as they can be.)"

Don't identify your product or service. (If you do, you'll be shunted to a lower level within seconds.) *Don't* use technical jargon in an attempt to confuse or intimidate the person on the other end of the line. You must without fail, however, use unmistakable VITO language that the secretary or receptionist will recognize as such. All the receptionist needs to shunt you over to Seymour is one syllable of feature- or function-speak! So don't talk like a Scymour. Talk like a VITO.

Now, let's say that in response to this last attempt, the receptionist says something like the following:

Receptionist: "Hey—are you trying to sell VITO a fax machine?" (Or, "Are you selling long-distance service?" Or, "Is this about office equipment?")

At this point, you've been stereotyped. The receptionist has mistaken you for the high-pressure, low-follow-through salesperson you've worked so hard not to be. Rather than explain the intricacies of the business partnership you're trying to establish, respond with something along these lines:

> *You:* "Let's get realistic. If all I wanted to do was get somebody to (buy a fax machine), I wouldn't need to talk to VITO, would I?"

In point of fact, you are trying to do much more than simply sell VITO (a fax machine). You want to work with VITO as a partner.

If the receptionist challenges you further, you have one last recourse for trying to get through during this call. Calmly and confidently say:

> "Would you knowingly stand in the way of Ms. Benefito's realizing the benefit that I just mentioned?"

145

OR:

> "Would you knowingly stand in the way of Widget Company's (gaining more market share)?"

OR:

> "Would you knowingly stand in the way of Ms. Benefito's (creating greater loyalty with existing customers)?

"Why Don't You Just Send Us Some Information?"

Whenever I hear this—and, thanks to the techniques I've just outlined, that's not very often—I say, "Certainly. I have a completely comprehensive and interactive package of information. If you stand it on its end, it's six feet one inch high, and it weighs 162 pounds. We call it Tony. When do you want me there?"

This line always gets a laugh. Use it if you're facing a real dead end. It may well get you past the gate and/or get you an in-person appointment..

"Can I Take a Message?"

> "Sorry, VITO's not in. Can I take a message?"

Some of your calls may reach this seeming dead-end—usually while you're talking to the receptionist, but possibly at other times as well. What do you do?

Say this: "Why, yes, thanks for asking! It's rather long, and it may take a few minutes. Have you got a big pad of paper handy? Or—you know what—I could save us both some time and get this important message out to VITO. What's VITO's fax number?"

You will get the fax number. In the extremely unlikely event that the person wants to take your verbal message, give your entire Opening Statement, including the ending question. Include specific times and days you'll be in the office for VITO's call. Then be there!

But let's be realistic. You can expect to obtain VITO's fax number in a flash by using this technique. With that number in hand, you will be ready to move on to the Fax Recovery. But before we look at that, let's talk for a moment about dealing with that other kind of gatekeeper: VITO's secretary or assistant.

Connecting with the Executive Suite: VITO's Secretary or Assistant

Many of the salespeople I work with are under the impression that dealing with this gatekeeper is significantly more complex and difficult than dealing with the front-line receptionist. Fortunately, they couldn't be more wrong.

Dealing with VITO's secretary or assistant is simplicity itself once you realize that this is the second most powerful person in the organization. Act on that assumption, and you'll be well on your way to building a business relationship that you can count on. Throw out the organization charts. Forget about the titles. This person knows as much about the goals, obstacles, and predispositions of this organization as anyone else. This person generally knows about changes in strategy and important business decisions *before* anyone other than VITO. This person is probably responsible, in large measure, for keeping VITO's little world from blowing up every day! This is a person you want—and must treat—as a powerful ally.

If you treat VITO's assistant as a minor functionary, someone incapable of comprehending the high-level message you have crafted for VITO, the doors will slam shut and, most likely, never open again. Treat VITO's assistant *as though he or she is speaking and acting for VITO* (which is, by the way, often quite literally the case), and the doors will swing open.

Give the Exact Same Opening Statement You Would Give to VITO

As you may already know, VITOs are never officially "in"—or at least that's how it seems.

When you've cleared the receptionist and VITO's secretary picks up the phone, I want you to picture this. VITO is dressed up in an official NASA-issue spacesuit. In fact, VITO has just blasted off the face of this earth and is now orbiting in the space shuttle! VITO's "out"—way, way out. So when you're talking to VITO's secretary, don't worry about VITO anymore.

Give the secretary or assistant the exact same opening statement you would give to VITO.

That's right. When you reach VITO's personal secretary or assistant, I want you to work through the Opening Statement in the exact same way you would if VITO were on the line. Pause for objections. Listen. Take notes. All of that. In other words, you are going to *talk to and treat this person as a VITO*, and you're going to mean it. Now, let me warn you: You can't do this if you have the slightest doubt about your ability to deal with the secretary or personal assistant as a business equal.

"Exactly like VITO?" Yes, exactly like VITO. The only adjustment you're going to make has to do with the beginning of your opening statement, your ending question, and the big three questions that follow. In these cases you will simply ask Tommie to speak for VITO.

That's it. That's the technique for turning around these supposedly fierce gatekeepers. And I'll tell you something: It works like gangbusters. All day long, secretaries of top decision makers across the country are forced to deal with people who don't acknowledge the pivotal role they play in attaining company goals. Your tactic is to *not be like those people*. Your tactic is to *assume that your contact can speak for VITO*. Nine times out of ten, you'll be right in that assumption, and the secretary, like VITO, will either forward your call to VITO or tell you when to call back for a telephone meeting.

In the overwhelming majority of cases—if you only remember not to patronize this person, to act with the same respect and deference you would accord VITO, to listen, listen, listen to what is being said— you will be successful.

Words to the wise: Once the business relationship is established, *always* keep the secretary involved in your efforts. You are not "using" anyone to "get to" anyone else; you are establishing a critical business alliance that should endure for as long as you have a business relationship with the organization.

Here's a story that will underscore the importance of treating VITO's secretary or assistant exactly like VITO. I was calling a VITO in New York City by the name of Joe Arthur; his secretary's name is Candy Overmeyer. I called at the appointed time; as it happened, Joe couldn't take my call because he was orbiting the earth in the space shuttle at the time. So when Candy answered the phone, I laid my Opening Statement on her. Candy said, "Did you send Joe a letter?"

I said, "Yes, I did. What did you think of it?" (*Not* "What did Joe think of it?") Then something magical happened. Candy said, "Well, Joe thought it was interesting that you focus on one thing, teaching people how to prospect for new business." And she proceeded to give me a blow-by-blow description of Joe's reaction to the letter.

I said, "Candy, is teaching your people to prospect for new business important to you?" Candy said, "Joe is concerned. We're coming out with a new product—and our people tend to go back to the same old accounts and neglect their prospecting work."

We went through the entire conversation this way. Finally, I asked, "Candy, what do you think we should do next?" Candy said, "Knowing Joe, I'll bet he's going to want to see an outline of your course." I said, "Candy, how many outlines would you like to see?" Candy answered, "Send back six—one for Joe and one for each of the five staff managers."

I sent Candy six outlines. Two weeks later I called her again and said, "Candy, this is Tony Parinello. What did you think of my outline?" Candy said, "Joe circled several things in your outline." And we went into an extended review of what Joe did and didn't like about my outline. After about ten minutes, I asked, "Candy, what do you think we should do next?" Candy said, "Knowing Joe, I think he'd want to have a few staff people sit in on one of your programs."

"Candy, that's going to be very difficult," I said, "because the programs I give are private corporate sessions. My customers don't like outsiders sitting in. But perhaps if you and Joe are getting together with the rest of the staff people, I could come in to give you a private two-hour presentation." I heard pages turning on Candy's desk calendar. Then I heard Candy say, "On June 14th, Joe will be having a meeting with all the vice presidents. Let me call you back." An hour later she called back and said, "Tony, you're on from ten to noon."

I never *once* asked Candy what Joe had to say about anything. I asked Candy what *Candy* had to say. And I got the appointment.

At the presentation, Joe himself, who at this point had never spoken to me, introduced me as follows: "Here's a guy whose expertise is prospecting for new business. He must be good, because he managed to book two hours of our time, and I've never even talked to him!" It went great. Twenty minutes into the presentation, Joe stopped me and said, "Tony, we'll take it." On the way out, after Joe had signed the contract, I stopped at Candy's desk, thanked her profusely, and promised to keep her informed at every step of the relationship. It was a promise I kept.

A few years later, I got a call from Candy. She told me she wanted me to know that Joe was leaving the company for another opportunity. Actually, as it turned out, it wasn't just Joe who was pursuing another opportunity. Joe was taking Candy with him. And you know who else he took with him? Me.

The Fax Recovery

The Fax Recovery is the technique to use if people tell you that VITO is in a meeting, out of town, on the way to a meeting, on the way to go out of town, or behind closed doors. (By the way, wouldn't you love to be able to sit in on one of these marathon, fate-of-the-Republic-hangs-in-the-balance meetings that always seem to happen just when you call? What do you suppose they're really talking about? Similarly, wouldn't you love to take a look inside that space shuttle they must always strap VITO into when you find out that VITO "just took off for the day" and thus can't take your call?)

There are two options to pursue in the event that VITO's gatekeepers or anyone else in the organization prevents you from getting through to VITO at the time you specify in your letter. In both cases, you must leave a message for VITO; both approaches involve use of the organization's fax number.

Option One: Send a Memo

But not just any memo! Did you ever see those little pink slips that fly around the office, the ones with "WHILE YOU WERE OUT" written across the top? You're going to take one of those, put it on the photocopier, and blow it up until it looks like it has a gland problem. It should occupy a full letter-size sheet of paper.

Put your neatly handwritten Opening Statement in the message area below the "WHILE YOU WERE OUT" headline. Include all the appropriate contact data in the spaces on the form, including your phone number. Fax it to VITO. Specify dates and times you'll be in the office for VITO's call. Be sitting by the phone at those times.

This is your cover sheet—don't dilute the effect by attaching a standard letter to this form.

When VITO steps off the space shuttle, passes through all the debriefings and the medical checks, and makes it back to the desk, there will be three piles on that desk. One will be incoming mail. Another will be incoming messages. And a third will be incoming faxes. Take a wild guess as to which one VITO's going to look at first. Right. The faxes. When VITO sees that big "WHILE YOU WERE OUT" slip that looks like it's on steroids, you will have earned a "Wow!" You will have earned Equal Business Stature.

Date _____   Time_____

WHILE YOU WERE OUT

M _____

of _____

Phone _____
Area Code   Number   Extension

TELEPHONED		PLEASE CALL	
CALLED FOR YOUR OPINION		WILL CALL AGAIN	
WANTS TO SEE YOU		PLEASE RETURN FAX	

Message _____
_____
_____
_____
_____
_____
_____
_____
_____
_____

Option Two: Send the Letter

Fax an exact copy of your letter to VITO with the "While You Were Out" message as the cover sheet. Cross out the Action P.S. and write in the margin, "Sorry I missed you." (This is the reason you must leave lots of open space in your letter to VITO.) Fax this. Then specify dates and times you'll be in the office for VITO's call. Be sitting by the phone at those times.

If Nobody Calls After You Send the Faxes, Do You Give Up and Move On?

Heck, no! Wait three days, then fax or call again with a new message. Make it creative and interesting. Talk about another testimonial or something else you've done to help another company in VITO's industry. Create a story line you can build on by adding a "third installment" if another message is required later.

If you fail to get a response by any of these methods, you can always ask the secretary for the number that will allow you to reach VITO's voice mail directly.

Getting VITO's Attention by Voice Mail

This is an excellent opportunity to speak directly to VITO on your own terms and, usually, for as long as you like. But you must be prepared! A voice mail system is an unforgiving thing, and if you sputter, repeat yourself, or trail off into silence there's usually no way to call the message back. You only have to be burned in this way once to know that voice mail is not a communications method designed for the salesperson who wants to wing it.

Have you ever flown in a glider? When you're coming in for a landing, if you don't line up properly with the runway, you're in big trouble. It's not like a small plane; you can't add power, pull back up, and take another approach. You get one shot at leaving that compelling voice mail message for VITO.

Take the time to develop a written version of your message before calling. You might choose to adapt an earlier message, but your best bet would probably be to develop a brand new success story and *deliver it with passion*. Consider this example.

Mr. Benefito, Will Prosper at XYZ. There is *so much excitement here* about what Mammoth Motor Company has accomplished! Would you believe that, right now, we are saving Mammoth Motor Company an average of $600,000 *per quarter*? Jack Ryan over at Mammoth told me, and this is a direct quote, now, "I have never seen anything like this system. It's a lifesaver for the production department. Please don't show it to my competitors." Well, Jack's competitors are shaking their heads at what we've done. Yes, that's a big number and at first we were surprised, too. But Mammoth has proved it quarter after quarter. These results may be hard to duplicate or exceed. You are probably very busy, but if you would like to discuss this further, I'll be at my desk waiting for your call anytime on Wednesday morning, between eight and twelve. Or have Tommi give me a call if I've picked an inconvenient time. The number here is 617/555-1212. Thanks for listening to my long message. I sincerely look forward to talking with you. My number is 617/555-1212.

The basic rule for voice mail is this: If you can't make the message come alive, don't leave it. Your message must be exciting to listen to. It must stop VITOs in their tracks. If you do it right, VITO will call just to see what kind of person would actually be brave enough to leave such a message. Work out a script; deliver it into your tape recorder and have your sales manager critique it. Work everything out well ahead of time. And remember, the last words out of your mouth in any voice mail message should be an expression of thanks, an "I look forward to speaking with you" statement, and your telephone number.

Again, *do not* leave a standard, boring answering-machine message. Remember, VITOs like people who can get excited. That's because too many of the people who work with VITO are too intimidated to get excited. Be the exception!

I was hired by Data Products Corporation to do a keynote speech for their sales convention on the strength of one compelling, passionate, high-energy, impossible-to-ignore voice mail message. I left the message for the executive vice president of sales for that company. He heard it, loved what I had to say, and called me up to offer the assignment. My cost of sales on that booking was about a dollar twenty-eight! If you want to take a quantum leap in your business relationship with VITO, shorten your sales cycle, and lower your cost of sales, leave a stirring, unforgettable voice mail message. You'll get a call back.

Some people talk about "making a good first impression"—and then leave phone messages that sound like they were delivered from the depths of a Sominex binge! Often, your phone message *is* your first impression. Treat it as such. Remember, you're on a job interview—and you can't afford to be ignored.

How's It Look?

If you execute all of the ideas in this chapter and find that you are still having difficulty getting through to and scheduling appointments with the VITOs you target, there is probably something wrong with either your delivery or the product or service you are offering. If it's the former, please review the steps for telephone success at the end of chapter eleven. You may find that you must revamp the way you are emphasizing benefits to VITO. (By the way, it's healthy to keep switching the benefits you highlight for the new VITOs you encounter. It keeps you from falling into a rut.)

Sidetracked with Seymour?

A little later in the book, we'll be looking at the techniques you'll use for success during the in-person meeting with VITO. In the next chapter, however, we'll examine a strategy you can use to get through to VITO if you find yourself, for whatever reason, dealing with Seymour—the person to whom salespeople are usually relegated when someone in the organization wants to stop the sales cycle dead in its tracks.

Chapter Thirteen:
The Pigeonholing Problem

Suppose you've already started your sales cycle with a Seymour. You've done your analysis, collected all the data, bought a lunch or two, maybe sprung for doughnuts and coffee in the morning, visited a few sites, made a few demos, and now you're going in to give your presentation to Seymour. You're expecting to meet with Seymour and perhaps one or two associates, but often, when you actually make your way into the building, you find that there are six or seven Seymours waiting to greet you. (My theory is that Seymours multiply like coathangers when you're not looking, but I could be wrong.) You give your presentation; it's one of the best presentations you've ever given in your life. All the Seymours are smiling and nodding their heads. You have few questions to answer, and the ones that do come up are easy. You get to the last slide; you put it up on the overhead projector and make your closing comments; you turn off the machine; flip on the lights; and you say to the head Seymour, "Seymour, as you can see, the facts are all here. Are you ready to work with us?" Then Seymour hesitates for a moment and says, "Well, I've got to see some more figures. We're talking to some other people. We have to crunch all the numbers on this end. Give me thirty days."

Bewildered, you walk from the conference room and out of the building. You get in your car and head back to your office. And you ask yourself, "How long is this going to last? How on earth do I turn up the heat under Seymour?" You get an idea—something that will necessitate another set of slides, but you can live with that—and you call Seymour the minute you walk in your office. But Seymour's not in.

And Seymour doesn't return your call that afternoon. Or the next day.

You call again the next day. Seymour's very busy.

After all your work, you're on the outside looking in again.

I'll bet you that this all sounds horribly familiar. I've just described the classic gridlock, the "I-loved-you-before-but-I'm-not-sure-if-I-still-love-you-now" problem we face all too often with Seymours.

When Seymour has either stalled you for the last two or three months (or years), or has simply given up on you and will not return your phone calls, you are, in a word, pigeonholed.

You want to get to VITO. You know that if you could, you would probably break through the logjam in the course of a single meeting. (VITOs, as you have probably gathered by now, aren't big on wasting their own time or that of anyone else in the organization, and are big on straight-ahead assessments of whether it is worthwhile to do business with someone.) How do you talk to the person who can make things happen for you—without appearing to go over Seymour's head?

The Pigeonhole Recovery Letter

Right now, we're going to take a look at a letter you and your sales manager can put together. If you follow the procedures I outline, this letter can get you out of the pigeonhole and into VITO's office. It won't make anyone angry or leave you looking underhanded.

Important note! The letter you'll see in this chapter is industrial-strength stuff, but it will *not make sales materialize where none would otherwise exist*. It will simply deliver the same result you would have gotten anyway from Seymour—but a lot sooner. If you were going to win the deal, you'll win it in a hurry. If you were going to lose the deal, you'll lose it in a hurry.

If you follow my instructions carefully, you will not jeopardize your relationship with Seymour.

What's the Goal?

The Pigeonhole Recovery Letter's aim is to either open up the relationship by pointing you toward VITO's office—or smoke Seymour out and help you determine that you're looking at an account that simply isn't worth pursuing anymore, no matter how much Seymour is enjoying all those free lunches and big colored charts. The letter really works. I know, because it's worked countless times for me. The *reason* it works is a simple one. Rather than *fighting* with Seymour, the Pigeonhole Recovery Letter allows you to move up the chain by making *heros* out of Seymours—if they can handle it.

As a practical matter, this letter will be written by you. But your manager will sign it, and others in your organization will approve it. Like the letter you developed for VITO, this one must make use of a Headline Statement showing the benefits of the proposed solution. This Headline Statement, however, *must* be a quote, and it must be signed *by a person in your own organization who outranks both you and your sales manager.*

Exactly who this person is depends on the relative importance of the VITO you're after. If the organization represents a multi-million-dollar account your firm's president has been salivating over, tracking down the president to approve the quote probably won't be too tough. In other instances, a quote from a regional vice president or other high-ranking officer may be more appropriate.

The first step is to consult with your manager about the proposed letter. The idea here is that, after signing and sending the letter, your manager—not you—will conduct the follow-up call referred to in the Action P.S. at the bottom of the page.

Once you've secured your organization's cooperation on this (and it shouldn't be too hard), develop a Headline Statement referring to initial work you have done in collaboration with Seymour. The quote will indicate that this work has identified a specific, quantifiable solution to a problem in VITO's organization.

For the Pigeonhole Recovery letter to work, it *must* feature Seymour's name in the Headline Statement. Other than that, it's just about identical in form to the standard letter for a first-time contact with VITO.

Here's an example of a Pigeonhole Recovery Letter that works.

**"Seymour Jones and my team have completed an
in-depth study. The results show that your
corporate personnel costs can be reduced by
36%—over $18,500 returned to your bottom line
annually."**

Jim Smith
President, XYZ

December 14, 1994

Mr. VITO Benefito
President

Dear Mr. Benefito:

Your Widget Department Specialist, Seymour Jones, has
been working with my account manager, Will Prosper.
We've studied your business. We understand your unique
needs. We're prepared to take action.
These are three of the many benefits we have provided
for other customers:

- An average 16% reduction in quarterly
  unemployment claims.

- Absentee rates at or below 5% within two
  months.

- In the words of Mary Jackson of Ellis
  Enterprises, "a staggering increase in the
  efficiency of support staff."

We stand ready to move forward with the solutions to
your personnel cost containment problems.

Sincerely,

Joan King
Sales Manager
555-1244

P.S.: I will call your office at 9:30 a.m. on Monday,
December 19. If you will not be in, please ask Tommie
to advise me of a more convenient time.

The Pigeonhole Recovery Process: Protocol and Diplomacy

Now, you never send a Pigeonhole Recovery Letter to VITO without inviting Seymour to take a look at it first. Call, fax, or leave a message for Seymour. Say something to this effect: "Hi, Seymour. My manager is getting ready to send a letter to your president. It has your name at the very top of it. I'd like to share it with you before it's mailed. Please call."

If Seymour knows the name of the health club you work out at every night, he'll be there waiting for you. If Seymour knows where you live, he'll be in your driveway when you get home that evening.

When Seymour returns your call asking to see the letter, be as polite as Emily Post would require—but don't get into the details of the letter. Instead, fax it or hand-deliver it. See what happens.

If Seymour likes the letter but wants you to hold on to it for a week or two, you've got a good sign. Seymour is probably interested in taking action, but too busy to do so. You can either wait (which may be understandable if you're dealing with a potentially large account), or say something like this: "Seymour, I understand your concern on this, but I can't wait forever. My manager has been asked by our V.P. to write all of our best prospects. Everybody reports to somebody, right? I'll tell you what, though. If I play my cards right, I may be able to stall her for 48 hours. I'll see what I can do." The result: You will probably get an up-or-down decision in short order.

If Seymour responds *negatively*, with something like "I don't want this letter to be mailed!", you have two choices. You can stop the letter and be right back where you started, or you can say something like this: "You know, Seymour, I really don't think I *can* stop my manager. If you and I don't want it to go out, you might have to call my boss and tell her not to send it." (The wording there is important: "If *you and I* don't want it to go out . . . .") Now, Seymour probably won't call your manager—in which case the letter goes out to VITO—but if a call does come through, your manager should be prepared to tell Seymour about the "pre-sales" dollars your company has spent on pursuing this opportunity—what with all the lunches, demos, analyses, and demonstrations— and the necessity of making a business decision on what action to take next. Your manager should then offer Seymour the opportunity to join in a three-way conference call with VITO.

If Seymour *ignores* messages from you about your plan to send the letter, you can either continue your attempts to reach Seymour (which probably won't get you anywhere), or simply send the letter to VITO, with a copy going out to Seymour as well.

If Seymour calls you in hysterics after the letter arrives on VITO's desk, you might decide to do a Say What: "Say *what*? My manager sent *what*? Oh, I'm so sorry . . . hey, Seymour, what can I say, I can't control what my manager does. I thought she'd wait until you and I could talk! We know how it is, Seymour—everybody reports to somebody, right? Listen, Seymour, my manager is an animal. I've seen her on the grill before. She doesn't stay there for long." Now, maybe this does represent a *teensy* white lie—and you may decide that it won't be appropriate with the Seymour you're trying to get a decision out of. Then again, if you've reached this stage of the sales cycle, and Seymour won't do you the simple courtesy of telling you that, no, there's no point in pursuing things any further, you may conclude that you'll still be able to sleep at night after using this technique.

Before Your Manager Follows Up with VITO by Telephone or in Person . . .

Give your manager all the paperwork you have on the initial call to VITO, including the ending question and the three big questions that follow. Ask your manager to try to arrange a meeting *for you* with VITO. At the conclusion of the conversation, your manager might say something like, "VITO, would you like to meet our account rep, who has been working with Seymour to uncover all of these savings?"

If VITO says yes, you can then tell Seymour that your manager has arranged a meeting between you and VITO—and that Seymour's really going to look like a hero when you get your solution implemented. (Which, of course, is quite true.)

Nailing Things Down

The technique described in this chapter will, in most cases, either get someone from your firm, preferably you, into VITO's office—or help you isolate and stop working on an account that's going nowhere. That last option might not seem like much of a blessing, but it is. After all, the point of this system is not to get sidetracked with Seymour, but to spend the lion's share of your time identifying and speaking to new VITOs.

I admit that this technique is not for the faint of heart. The Pigeon-hole Recovery Letter is a tactic that should be used sparingly. If you send them out too often, you'll send the message to others in your own organization that you can't conclude your sales calls, and that you're consistently calling too low in the organization. Once again, let me warn you never to send anyone a Pigeonhole Recovery Letter without first securing the approval of all the people in your organization whose names appear in it.

If the account turns out not to come your way, so be it. Once you finalize where all your pigeonholed accounts really stand, you can focus all your efforts on prospecting to the top person in the organization.

CHAPTER FOURTEEN:
THE IN-PERSON MEETING—AND SOME POSSIBLE OBJECTIONS

By now you're primed to meet VITO by telephone or in person. You understand the Influence and Authority Network; you've learned how to build rapport and achieve Equal Business Stature by focusing on solutions. You've developed your first-call objectives and your initial letter to VITO, including that all-important Opening Statement.

But wait! What if VITO tries to shunt you over to Seymour? What if VITO is absolutely in love with another supplier? What if VITO is impressed enough with your call and letter to ask you to come in for a brief meeting—but won't even give you the time of day once you show up? What on earth are you supposed to *say* to VITO once you show up?

We'll be addressing all those issues—and the ever-popular topic of dealing with objections that arise during the sales cycle—in this chapter.

A Brief Story about the Perils of "Breaking the Ice" with VITO

I once had a *ten-minute appointment* scheduled with a top executive at a large manufacturing firm. I'm not kidding—my appointment was for between 1:00 and 1:10 PM.

Now we've already touched on the idea that being "on time" for VITO means being a few minutes early. So I was five minutes early, sitting on the couch outside of this huge hand-carved mahogany door. At precisely 1:00, the door opened, and my contact, Harry Wall, stepped out, shook my hand, and led me into his office. He sat down behind a massive mahogany desk, and on the wall behind him was a magnificent framed photo—about three feet high and about six feet wide—of a long, elegant racing sloop speeding across a bay somewhere. Emblazoned on the sail of that boat are the words "WALL STREET." I put two and two together and realized that I'm looking at a photo of this man's personal racing boat.

After we'd exchanged pleasantries, I decided I'd do the textbook "icebreaker" maneuver. I said, "Mr. Wall, that's a very impressive racing sloop. Tell me, does it have running or fixed back stays?" He launched into a ten-minute discussion about the boat—how it was constructed, how many races he'd won, where he'd competed. And then, at the end of his discourse, he glanced at his watch, looked at me, and says, "Sorry, Tony. We're out of time. I have to run." He walks out of the office and leaves me sitting in front of his desk. I had just blown the ten most important minutes of the sales cycle listening to Mr. Wall talk about his yacht.

I never did get another appointment with Harry Wall. Later I learned that someone else had sold him the exact computer system I was trying to discuss with him. From that day forward, I have *never* used an "icebreaker" question to begin a meeting with a VITO. Not once. And I've never regretted it, either.

No matter what any other book may tell you about this, don't try to "break the ice" with VITOs. Get right down to business and talk about your record and your solutions. When you're done talking business, and you're on your way out, that's the time to make chitchat and end on a positive personal note.

What's Really on VITO's Mind?

You need to be prepared for anything and everything VITO can throw at you during that first face-to-face meeting. To be in the best possible position to react to the questions and challenges that will be coming your way, you'll have to take a closer look at the way VITO thinks.

VITO—like others within the Influence and Authority Network—has a personal agenda relating to business decisions and actions. The origins of that agenda can be found in the surrounding circumstances VITO faces at any given time: the current financial status of the business, recent moves by competitors, future goals, personal considerations, and, perhaps most important, what VITO perceives and believes about the world as a result of past experience.

Not surprisingly, VITO is going to tend to move toward things that seem to advance items on that personal agenda—and away from things that are seen as obstacles to those items. In fact, at any given time, VITO is likely to be moving either *toward a positive outcome* or *away from a negative outcome.* (No, VITOs don't usually stand still!) You must be in a position to understand which direction VITO is moving in—and why—during your encounters, so you can chart your own proper parallel course.

The Four Mindsets

You are likely to find VITO (indeed, you are likely to find anyone in the organization) in any number of different mindsets. At this point, we're going to examine the four most popular ones. Your own experience within your industry may give you some further insights. Of course, your overriding goal when communicating with VITO is to determine which mindset is currently predominant and adjust your approach accordingly.

What follows is broadly applicable to phone encounters with VITO, as well as in-person meetings. A word of warning seems appropriate before we examine these four mindsets. You can't assume that VITO's attitude on any given issue is necessarily shared by others in the Influence and Authority Network. Where VITO sees potential (in expanding into a new market, for instance), Seymour and others in the organization may well see only danger and problems (in the form of increased production rates, shortened production cycles, conversion problems with existing software, and a host of other issues).

This is an extremely important point. *A goal for VITO is not necessarily a goal shared by others in the organization.* We may be used to thinking in terms of VITO defining the broad mission statement for the company, and this is certainly accurate enough, but it's a big mistake to assume that *all* of VITO's goals are shared by others in the Influence and Authority Network. Similarly, something VITO perceives as a victory—say, a proposed update of technology that will streamline a bloated organization—may be viewed as a potential catastrophe by others you come in contact with. As a general rule, the higher the person is in the organization, the more likely that person is to share in VITO's perception of what constitutes a "win." Managers and directors tend to see things in generally the same ways that VITO does; Seymours and consumers typically do not.

That having been said, the necessity of *finding out* how VITO is thinking about the ideas you're discussing remains. When you ask VITO something along the lines of, "Mr. Benefito, what are your goals for the widget department over the next three months?", pay very close attention to the answer you get. It will almost certainly point you toward one of the following categories.

Mindset One: Opportunity

In this mindset, VITO is open to new ideas. The thought process runs something like this: "All right; our next step is to capture the Asian market for our widgets. How do we make that happen? What do we need to do to make sure that it happens by the end of the fourth quarter?"

Typically, this mindset arises when things are going well. Perhaps new products have been released and are meeting with some initial success in the market. Perhaps VITO's company has increased its market share. Perhaps the new mission statement has lit a fire under everyone in the organization. VITO is moving *toward a positive*.

You're in a great position! VITO's looking for new ways to achieve goals, and is perhaps on the lookout for the edge that will strengthen the company's position even more.

Here are your goals for a conversation with a VITO who is in the Opportunity mindset.

- Support and nurture the current mindset.
- Help VITO understand how the total solution you and your company have to offer translate into *specific benefits* that will advance VITO's present and future mission.
- Take this opportunity to sell *expanded solutions* with *near-term add-on potential.* (In other words, take advantage of the fact that the Opportunity mindset is the best one in which to establish the framework for an ongoing partnership with VITO.)
- Be prepared for an average or slightly-longer-than-average sales cycle. VITO is not in a crisis mode, and is likely to want to take all the time necessary to make a solid decision. VITO will likely want to check all the angles before signing up with a new business partner who is capable of fulfilling future growth plans.
- Remember that price will *not* typically be a major issue.

Mindset Two: 911

Put out the fire! In this mindset, VITO is trying to correct a crisis situation. The thought process runs something like this: "We're losing ground here."

Maybe the competition is getting an edge. Maybe the economy is sour. Maybe the customer base is shrinking. Whatever the emergency, VITO is dialing 911 and reaching for the nearest extinguisher. VITO is moving *away from the negative result* of a pressing problem.

Here are your goals for a conversation with a VITO who is in the 911 mindset.

- Recognize that a crisis almost always prompts the need to fix this particular problem *now*. Focusing on just about anything else will not win you any points with VITO at this stage. Don't pursue fancy proposals, endless studies, full-blown analyses, or anything else. Sell the scaled-down solution to the crisis at hand, period. (Remember: When the bell rings, firemen don't talk much; they *act*.)

- Recognize that a crisis sometimes dictates buying for price and buying *fast*. And if you've been selling for very long at all, you probably already know that selling on price is a way to establish a *short-term* business relationship—one that is likely to end when a lower price comes along.

- Recognize that a crisis often necessitates rapid decision making, and an accompanying acceleration of the sales cycle. This means that VITO may not be taking all factors or potential later disadvantages into account. You must move faster than your competition and be up-to-date with exactly what that competition is offering.

- Upgrade the relationship once a solution is found. After you hand VITO the fire extinguisher, you should never walk away and consider the sale closed. (Remember, we don't close VITO. We open doors!) If you help VITO solve this problem, you will have earned a good measure of loyalty and respect. Immediately after the fire is out, return with your long-term solutions. VITO will probably revert to the Opportunity mindset, and may become open to learning the total scope of your solutions.

Mindset Three: "All Set"

In this mindset, VITO is trying to save time by sticking with an existing vendor or supplier—but the conviction that the vendor or supplier is the best partner is not etched in stone. The thought process goes something like this: "Hey, I've got no needs. I believe my current source of supply is taking care of everything." After all, If VITO or his people walked through what every potential vendor or supplier had to offer, nothing would ever get done.

Here are your goals for a conversation with a VITO who is in the "All Set" mindset.

- Understand that VITO's *believing* the company is "all set" with the current source is not the same thing as VITO's being *convinced* the company is "all set" with that source.

- Be willing to professionally but firmly challenge VITO's "all-set" opinion. (We'll look at this in more detail later on.)

- Know the difference between this mindset and the next one, in which there is little or no chance of establishing a business partnership with VITO.

Mindset Four: No Daylight

In this mindset, VITO is set in a firm conviction that the current vendor or supplier is the right one for the organization. Unshakable loyalty exists. The mindset goes something like this: "I've spent a good deal of time looking into this and I've studied all the angles. We've made the best choice, and our current team has it handled. I'm convinced we're going in the right direction already."

In this instance, VITO or someone VITO trusts has gone to the trouble to determine that the current vendor or supplier is definitely the one to stay with.

You are extremely unlikely to win this VITO's account. However, if you want to try making a presentation, it probably can't hurt.

Here are your goals for a conversation with a VITO who is in the "No Daylight" mindset.

- Expect a very long interest-building cycle before the sales cycle begins in earnest.

- Try convincing VITO that you have a better solution by broadcasting your very best references, and by passing along, very slowly and skillfully, a large number of staggering testimonials from customers who are willing to back up what you are saying by talking to VITO on the phone.

- Invite VITO to various business events. Expose VITO to the other VITOs who are your loyal customers.

- Arrange to be awarded a Congressional Medal of Honor if you eventually win this VITO's account. In the vast majority of cases, it will not happen even if you follow the steps just outlined.

Remember—There Are Two Categories Here

On the one hand, you may be dealing with the VITOs who head up companies in your *existing customer base*. On the other hand, you may be dealing with VITOs who lead organizations that you have never contacted before.

For the first group, your aim is to quantify and broadcast the continuing benefit—preferably in dollar terms—of doing business with you. For the second group, your aim is to *listen* for current requirements, and then to highlight your past successes and explore the possibility of a mutually beneficial business partnership.

Most of what follows is designed to help you make the most of your meeting with VITOs at companies you have not yet worked with. We'll talk more about VITOs at your current accounts a little bit later.

The First Few Seconds

You've probably heard it a thousand times: You don't get a second chance to make a first impression. If that's true in business in general, it's doubly so in dealing with VITOs, especially ones that represent potential new accounts for you. What do you do to make sure that you stand out from the pack as a different kind of business professional when you first make it into VITO's office?

You may remember that I came down very strongly against using company stationery or other identifying material in your initial letter to

VITO. That was a letter—this is a meeting. Now is the *perfect* time to use your company logo to advantage. Here's what you do.

During your first meeting with VITO, pass along a three-ring binder with your company logo on the front. You might decide to make the first page a copy of your initial letter, or of any other correspondence you have sent along before this point. Explain that your gift to VITO has a practical purpose. You'll be sending along updates on your progress with others in the organization on a regular basis—and VITO can include each within the binder. This is a very strong, highly professional way to begin your first meeting with both VITOs at companies you have not yet worked with and those in your current customer base. Taking this approach will automatically distinguish you from the vast majority of salespeople VITO has met with.*

So. You walk in the door. You look VITO in the eye. You say, "Mr. Benefito, it's great to finally meet you." Shake hands firmly and confi-

---

* There is another method *exclusively* for use in first meetings with VITOs in existing accounts. This is an existing account to which you've been delivering some undeniable hard-dollar (say, lower production costs) and soft-dollar (say, improved employee morale) results. Order a custom-made coffee cup that prominently features your company logo and colors. I find a large executive-size cup and a matching coaster, works best. You'll probably spend fifteen dollars on this, but believe me, it will be money well spent.

Attach a small tag to this item. On this tag, detail the measurable, quantifiable savings that you've been able to achieve in VITO's company. Wrap the cup in a little box and give it to VITO as an introduction present. When VITO unwraps it right then and there and sees the beautiful cup, you'll probably see a smile and hear something like "What's this?" That's when you say, "VITO, working with Seymour, we've been able to quantify that our business relationship has (saved you X dollars over the last X years)." And you will have planted a permanent "silent sales rep" that will sit on VITO's desk for the length of your partnership.

Here's a powerful illustration of how anchoring your results to a coffee cup in this way really can make a huge difference in the way VITO perceives your organization. One rep I know, named Frank, gave VITO the cup after having implemented his company's program. The tag on the handle read, "Increased production for third quarter: Net Benefit to Benefito Industries, $650,000." That cup stuck around the office for a good long while, a constant reminder of exemplary performance. But the story gets better! The rep made a routine visit to VITO *three years later* and noticed that the handle on the cup had broken. VITO had glued it back on. "VITO," Frank said, "why don't you let me get you another cup?" VITO said, "Don't you dare touch that. That's my $650,000 cup!" Imagine—three years later, and VITO still remembered!

dently, pumping only two or three times. You pass along your notebook. What next?

Beyond the First Few Seconds: Opening Your Business Conversation with VITO

VITO is usually rushed. Don't be discouraged. Be like VITO: brief and to the point. Whether on the phone or during an in person meeting, exchange an initial pleasantry and proceed to your Opening Statement. As always, pace yourself so that VITO can interrupt you and do the talking. When VITO talks, *listen and take notes.*

In general, follow all the rules for phone contact with VITO that were outlined in chapter eleven.

■   ■   ■

"I don't have much time. What's on your mind?"

Regardless of which of the four mindsets your VITO is in when you encounter each other, and regardless of whether you're talking on the telephone or meeting in person, you're likely to hear something like these two sentences at the outset of your exchange.

First of all, remember those two big fears VITO has about salespeople. You must not waste time. And you must not ask VITO idiotic questions.

- "Who's your long distance carrier?"
- "How much have you spent on overseas calls this quarter?"
- "Are your people happy with their office equipment?"
- "Do you have a service contract on your copiers?"
- "How long have you been buying floppy disks made in Pakistan?"

VITO doesn't know the answer to these questions, and if you ask them you'll be seen as a challenge to VITO's authority.

"What Happens After I Say My Opening Statement?"

Following are some examples of different conversations that could conceivably follow your Opening Statement. Parts that must be customized to your selling environment are set apart (in parentheses).

The following conversations are provided as guidelines only! Please do not attempt to march lockstep through the conversation, with these conversations as your "scripts." It won't work. VITO never knows the lines! And keep in mind that your conversation will last only as long as VITO wants it to last. VITO is in complete control; all you can do is influence the conversation with the proper questions and answers, and stay away from features and functions—the "F" words that will cause VITO to automatically disconnect from your conversation.

Opening Statement Response #1: "I'm Interested"

> *VITO:* You know, we were just talking about that this morning at our staff meeting. It sounds great. Tell me all about it!

Sounds like a dream come true, doesn't it? Be careful!

At seminars, when I ask salespeople to tell me how they'd respond to this request of VITO's, there are two answers that come up more often than any others. The first is, "Press for an appointment. Tell VITO you'll be in the area on Monday morning at 8:00, and ask if that's a good time. After all, if he's that interested, he'll want to spend some time with you to discuss it." The second is, "Tell VITO everything about the product, service, or solution. After all, you've just been asked to tell VITO all about it!" Both of these answers represent big problems for you if you follow through on them!

Meeting with VITO is great, and there's a time and a place to do it—but your objective is to get VITO to tell you to come in, not the other way around. As for going all-out on a description of your product, service, or solution, *you just don't know enough* about VITO yet to do that. Remember, we salespeople tend to talk too much, particularly during phone encounters. Sometimes it's hard to tell if what we're passing along is really engaging VITO and addressing the needs of the organization, and sometimes we stray from our objective of discussing benefits with VITO, and fall into the trap of discussing features. So to avoid that, I'm going to suggest that you resist the temptation to do a "product dump" at this stage.

Here's what I want you to say when you hear VITO say something like "Tell me all about that (product/service/solution) of yours."

> *You:* What is it you want to know about our (product/serv-
> ice/solution)?

When you say that, VITO is in a position to tell *you* what's of in-
terest. And you'll find out what they talked about at that staff meeting!
VITO's talking, VITO's got the control. You're listening and taking notes.
But what if, in response to this question, you hear something like this?

> *VITO:* You're the expert. Take it from the top. I want to hear
> everything.

If VITO says that to you, give VITO a choice of three things to talk
about, attach a time line, and then follow along. This brings us to an
important call objective: determining VITO's goals, plans, and objectives
over a particular period of time. But you don't do this by asking, "VITO,
what are your company's goals for this year?" That's much too vague.
VITO isn't going to take time to educate you about all that! Instead, try
this approach.

> *You:* VITO, the other (manufacturing clients) that I deal with
> tell me that these three things are of paramount impor-
> tance to them. In the next quarter, will you be focusing
> on . . .

Then you list for VITO no more than three *benefits you are able
to deliver to others in VITO's industry.* Here's another example of what
it might look like.

> *You:* Our (retail customers) say they're focused on (increasing
> employee effectiveness, consolidating operations, and as-
> suring the highest level of customer retention and satis-
> faction). Are you looking at any of these areas in the
> (next quarter)?

These three things may in fact be the same three things that are
listed in your letter. But they *must be benefits.* Stay away from features

at all costs! If VITO picks one, go into more detail *about that benefit*, citing success stories from your company's past where appropriate.

Let's say that you lay out three benefits, A, B, and C—and VITO says none of them are of interest. Don't throw out another three! Ask for VITO's guidance one more time.

> *VITO:* What you just outlined is not what we're focusing on here next quarter.

> *You:* Well, there are a lot of other areas we could be looking at. What will you be focusing on next quarter?

Opening Statement Response #2: "Oh? How Do You Do That?"

Suppose you begin to move toward your success stories, but VITO cuts you off at the pass.

> *You:* Mr. Benefito, we've done a lot of work with companies in your industry, and I think we have a new way to get your product to market quicker without sacrificing quality.

> *VITO:* Oh? How do you do that?

Be careful! Don't lecture VITO on features over the phone. In person, you can monitor reactions more closely, but over the phone, you'll have no idea how VITO is reacting to what you have to say.

Features bore most VITOs to tears. I make it a personal rule never to mention features to a VITO during an initial phone contact, and only to do so in person after I have seen persuasive evidence that I am dealing with a VITO who has a genuine Seymour outlook on the world. These are pretty rare, but they are out there. Otherwise, I stick with benefits and, if those seem to have made an impression, the related advantages. (You might want to take this opportunity to review one of the Network of Influence and Authority charts featured earlier in this book. Feel free to draw an arrow from the BENEFIT part of the chart to the AD-VANTAGE part of the chart—and draw a vertical line to the right of the FEA-TURE part of the chart. This will help you remember that it's always permissible to move from a benefit to an advantage in talking to a VITO on the phone, but very dangerous indeed to talk about features.)

If you're pressed on this point during a telephone conversation, you could tell VITO that you have people on your staff who handle the technical parameters, and that if VITO likes, you can have them drop by for a quick briefing with VITO's technical staff. Talk about Equal Business Stature!

Alternatively, you could tell VITO that a technical discussion will require several charts and spec sheets, and that the resulting conversation may last upwards of fifteen or twenty minutes. Then conclude by saying, "If you want, I can have someone here fax the specs to you directly. There's about four or five pages, and we should use them as source documents, because this could get into a somewhat lengthy technical discussion." I guarantee you, this will refocus the discussion.

Stay on benefits and advantages and you will never go wrong.

Opening Statement Response #3: "But You're Not the Lowest Price"

> *VITO:* I've heard you guys are not the lowest price in town, and I always buy the lowest price.

Note: What comes next takes unshakable confidence, but do it anyway.

> *You:* VITO, could you please define "price"?
>
> *VITO:* What do you mean by that? "Price" means the lowest number.
>
> *You:* Well, others in (VITO's industry), such as (use specific names), have defined "price" as . . .

Be prepared to provide examples of how your other customers in VITO's industry have defined price. "Mr. Benefito, the other manufacturing clients, such as ABC Corporation, tell me that price includes higher effectiveness and better attitudes among key employees, especially as this relates to total quality management. Other elements of price I've heard about would be lower turnover and increased process control. Are these factors part of *your* price equation?" This approach would probably fail spectacularly with our binary friends, the Seymours. VITOs, however, will understand what you're getting at.

Opening Statement Response #4: "Sorry, Not Interested"

> *VITO:* I have no interest whatsoever in this.
>
> *You:* I really didn't expect you to have any interest. If you did, you would have called me!

Warning! This takes practice. You cannot run the risk of sounding sanctimonious or sarcastic. Here are two alternate approaches:

> *You:* It's not that surprising to me to hear you say that, Mr. Benefito. You know, most of the top people I talk to aren't interested until they realize exactly how we can become a partner in helping them achieve important goals for this (quarter/fiscal year/whatever).

OR:

> *You:* You know, it is amazing to me that I have the (2,000) customers that I do, Mr. Benefito. Because they *all* said they had no interest at first. But then they took the time to take a look at how we could help them with a few of their most important goals.

(Again, listen and take notes to whatever VITO says in response. If what VITO outlines leads you to believe your solution can in fact help, follow VITO's lead and supply appropriate success stories that are directly tied in to the problems he identifies. If your solution really can't help, but you know of another solution that can, by all means tell VITO about it! I call this *building value-added rapport*, and it turns VITOs into long-term business allies. You will probably have an open door to call VITO at a later date to find out whether or not VITO used your suggestion and how things worked out. Remember, you'll need business three months from now, too.)

Opening Statement #5: "It's Not My Priority Now"

> *VITO:* What you just said is not a current priority.

Retain your Equal Business Stature, then bail out. As a businessperson, you must be willing to accept that what you have to offer may not be at the top of VITO's list at this point in time. Ask one solid question, follow up, and back off.

> *You:* When do you feel this will become a priority—(one month, two months, three months) from now?
>
> *VITO:* (Perhaps peeved by your persistence.)
>
> *You:* (Very conversational.) I apologize for being so bold, Mr. Benefito, but we've helped (44) other firms in your field to achieve (mention one or two of your very best benefits). Sometimes I get overly enthusiastic about giving everyone that edge. Maybe my solution isn't right for you at this time.

If you still get a negative reaction after an exchange such as this, odds are good that you are dealing with a VITO who is in a No Daylight mindset. Don't try to push; it won't work. Just disengage, thank VITO for the time, keep the contact active, and check in by phone or mail every now and then to see whether your message will be likely to be greeted with more interest.

Opening Statement Response #6: "I'm All Set, Thanks"

The following technique is for when you're trying to determine whether or not VITO's loyalty to the current supplier really is unshakable. Like much of the rest of this book, it's not for the faint of heart, and it does take unshakable confidence. But you may find that it works wonders for you.

> *VITO:* I'm extremely happy with my current source of supply. They take care of all our needs. I would never consider changing.
>
> *You:* Mr. Benefito, would you be interested in knowing what your loyalty is costing you? (Or: Would you be interested in knowing how much your loyalty is costing you?) (Or: Would you like to know if you're missing out on anything as a result of this loyalty?)

You've just challenged VITO's world. But you know what? VITO can take it. But you have to be ready for what's coming next; you have to be prepared with quantifiable results to back up your challenge.

> *VITO:* What do you mean by that? Even if my loyalty were costing me something, I'd never go through the nightmare of converting everything. All that time, effort, and energy counts for something, too.

Don't be vague in your response! Cite specific amounts that you have been able to save others in VITO's industry.

> *You:* Would it be worth ($22,000)? One of our customers found that loyalty to another supplier was costing them ($22,000) yearly in direct costs alone. Now, that's the hard dollars. There were soft dollar costs, too: (employee turnover, poor response rate to customer complaints, lapses in quality control). Mr. Benefito, would you like an opportunity to discover what your hard and soft savings could be?

(OR:)

> *You:* Mr. Benefito, the ABC company was able to (decrease their average time to market with new products by twelve percent) by working with us. I don't know how much your loyalty is costing you now—but would you be interested in going to the next step so we could find out exactly what your savings could be?

STOP TALKING! Wait for VITO's reply. It may take a while, and you may feel a powerful urge to fill in the gap in the conversation. Don't do it. Stand your ground and let VITO respond to this question . . . then follow VITO's lead. If you get a negative response, you are in all likelihood looking at a No Daylight mindset. But the conversation may well proceed along these lines:

VITO: What would it take to find that out? (Or: What are you talking about? How would you get that kind of information?) (Or: What is this "next step" you're talking about?) (Or: We don't plan on changing, but just out of curiosity, how would you go about finding something like that out?)

If you get any response along these lines from your challenge to VITO's loyalty, it will be the biggest sign of interest you'll ever get from someone who's said "not interested." You must be ready with the exact action plan that will help VITO determine how much that loyalty is costing. If you *cannot* lay out all of the steps of your action plan, do not challenge VITO's loyalty in the first place!

You: Well, Mr. Benefito, first I'll need (fifteen minutes) of your time to go over a few business issues, then (four hours) with (Seymour, the CFO, the manager of the department, whoever), then eight hours back in my office to put it together—and if we start today I can be back to you by (4:00 PM on Thursday) with a complete summary of the benefits and hard- and soft-dollar savings we can offer you.

Of course, where you see the information in parentheses, you should insert your own time frames. You must customize them to your own experience within the industry, and you must be able to stick to what you say. Don't ever promise VITO a five-minute meeting that can't be conducted in less than twenty.

Important Note! VITO's "How-would-you-find-that-out" question and your "Here's-what-I'll-need" response marks the successful outcome of your first visit with VITO! This exchange is the unspoken aim of *all* of these sales dialogues. Of course, you must first *wait* for VITO to ask you the question. Once you hear it, though, you should set out what you're looking for in a straightforward way, establish the dates and times, ask VITO the *broad* questions you need to ask, then get off the phone or out of VITO's office and get to work. It bears repeating that you must not at any stage of your relationship with VITO, and certainly not at this one, pepper VITO with questions about past contract history, specific prices, service contracts, or any other mundane details.

Opening Statement Response #7: "No Way You Can Help Me"

> *VITO:* I really doubt that you people can help with any of our corporate goals.

Important note: In dealing with this and other responses from VITO, remember that you're looking for base hits, not home runs. Highlight a specific, demonstrable benefit for VITO, even if it's not the kind of benefit that turns an industry upside down. The VITOs of the world today are looking in every corner of their organization for savings and increased efficiencies. Base hits—dollars, cents, minutes, seconds—count!

> *You:* The president of (Rogers International) initially questioned our ability to handle diverse tasks. She was surprised to see the real difference we made in cutting down on inventory without the worry of stock-outs.

STOP TALKING. If VITO does not respond within five seconds, proceed with something along these lines:

> *You:* Her results may be hard or even impossible to duplicate, but would you like to take the first step to find out if you might be able to realize a similar or even greater benefit?

Opening Statement Response #8: "I Know All About Your Company"

> *VITO:* I've heard of your company. We really have no interest in pursuing this.
>
> *You:* Mr. Benefito, do you not have the interest—or do you not have the time?

It's been my personal experience that there's a tremendous difference between not having interest and not having time. Highlighting the distinction may well win you a hearing. Both of these responses come from an initial misunderstanding on VITO's part as to the actual reason for your call and the benefits your solutions can offer. If you run into this objection time and time again, you should examine your opening statement more closely. (In the event, you may want to try to rescue the situation by saying something like, "VITO, maybe *I* didn't do a good enough job explaining exactly what this call/visit is about and what my company has to offer.")

Opening Statement Response #9: "Talk to Seymour"

You must master this response and overcome it if you want to sell to VITO. In all likelihood, you will find that this is the single most popular response to your opening statement.

You are not doing your job if you accept this shunt to Seymour without getting the answers you need.

> *VITO:* I'm way too busy to talk about this. I have people on my staff to look at these issues. You want to talk with Seymour Jones in our design and development group.

Whether VITO says something like the above during a call or an in-person meeting, you *must* find some way to salvage the situation. During a telephone call, this kind of response presents a particularly tough challenge, as VITO will be tempted to connect you to Seymour without asking you your opinion on the matter. If you let that happen, or if you let VITO steer you out of the office and toward Seymour's, you will not have accomplished your objectives. Try this.

> *You:* Before Seymour spends his valuable time and your company's money talking with me, let me ask you—what are you looking for in a business relationship?

Trust me. This is a show-stopper. Only VITO can answer this question; the response you get will give your business relationship with VITO two immediate and powerful benefits. First, you will quickly build Equal Business Stature by showing VITO that you understand the importance of conserving employee time and expense. Second, you will develop in-sights on how VITO makes decisions and looks at the issue of spending capital.*

"Here's What I Look for in a Business Relationship, But . . . "

I was granted fifteen minutes with the president and founder of one of the largest photo developing companies in the country. I had prepared for the meeting for days. What would I say? What would VITO say? How would the conversation flow? What should we discuss? Let me tell you here and now, this question about business criteria was not on my list.

Well, the time for my meeting rolled around, and I was escorted to the president's suite. (As you might imagine, this man's office had more than a few spectacular photographs on display, but having already learned my lesson on "icebreakers," I did not comment on any of them.) I sat down, ready to discuss the president's plans, goals, and ob-jectives for the upcoming year.

The meeting rolled along pretty smoothly. At the end of the fifteen minutes, the president shook my hand and started to walk me out the door. I stopped in the doorway, looked him in the eye, and said, "VITO, I want to thank you very much for giving me the opportunity to meet with you today, but I couldn't help noticing the painting over your cre-denza. Can I ask you what the significance of that painting is?"

It was a large oil painting of Jack Murphy Stadium in San Diego. The stadium was filled with people waving colorful flags and holding up

---

* The technique for adapting this to VITO's secretary or assistant should, at this point, come as no surprise. If VITO's secretary ever says that you're being trans-ferred to Seymour, say, "Before Seymour spends his valuable time and your com-pany's money talking with me, could you get VITO's answer to one question? What does VITO look for in a business relationship?" Trust me on this one too! Say it with conviction and a sense of responsibility, and this will prompt an *imme-diate* response from VITO's secretary, something like, "You mean you're not going to speak with Seymour until I get this question answered from VITO?" To which you can reply, "Well, wouldn't it be a shame if Seymour spent all his time with me only to find out that I'm not able to satisfy VITO's critical business require-ments?" Now you can have a very casual conversation with VITO's secretary about the importance of you and your organization totally understanding VITO's goals and exactly how VITO selects a business partner. It would almost be irre-sponsible to shunt you over to Seymour without nailing down this essential infor-mation!

banners. The bleachers were packed. In the foreground was a two-door 1961 Chevy Impala. The front wheels were off the ground, but the car was not moving forward. It was bouncing up and down. There was a man standing alongside one of the front wheels with a yardstick. Another man was leaning over, apparently to determine how high the car was bouncing.

It was a very strange painting.

The president said, "Tony, there's a contest here in San Diego. Car buffs set up their cars with hydraulic springs and compete to see whose car can bounce the highest."

And I asked, "Well, how does that fit in with your business?"

You know what the president said? He said, "Tony, I have a yardstick of my own. When people come into my office with new ideas, the person who registers the highest on my yardstick wins."

And it was then that I asked a VITO for the first time: "Could you please share with me the elements of your yardstick?" In other words, what exactly are you looking to measure with that yardstick?

We talked about his priorities for a solid forty-five minutes. This at the conclusion of my scheduled fifteen-minute meeting! I left that office knowing exactly what I would need to do to work with that VITO. In the months that followed, I focused on what he'd told me and nothing else. And I won that account.

When you ask VITO about the criteria for establishing a new business partnership, you may get an answer like this:

> *VITO:* Well, I look for a supplier/partner/business partner ready to take responsibility and solve problems. When a new solution becomes available, I want a pro-active team to be watching out for me and making sure that I'm getting the very best value and solution for my needs. In brief, I want new and creative ideas. I want a partner who's into total quality management. SO: Now that I've cleared that up for you, you'll want to talk to Seymour Jones, who makes all recommendations in this area for me.

STOP! You still can't let this happen until you've gotten your answer to the big question of whether or not VITO would do business with you.

If VITO tries again to shunt you to Seymour, you must keep this from happening.

Here's what to say.

> *You:* Mr. Benefito, if my company can measure up to your business criteria and satisfy Seymour's technical needs, could you picture yourself as one of our customers by (the end of the next quarter, the end of the fiscal year, or the end of some other, similarly specific time period)?

If VITO says no firmly and without reservation, you've got the ultimate qualifier. But this is rarer than you might think. After all, VITOs don't get to be VITOs by passing up opportunities! (They also don't tie up the time of key people in their organization by making them spend time with salespeople who don't offer something of value.) You are more likely to hear an answer like this:

> *VITO:* Well, we have a lot to discuss yet. But if you could satisfy my staff, and if I could get an edge using your solution, maybe I could see myself working with your organization. (Or: Well, I'm never one to pass up a good business opportunity, but I'm just not sure if you're right for us. It's too early to tell.)

Important note! Never ask VITO "why," especially if when you've been presented with vague statements like "just not sure" or "need to feel more comfortable" or "not certain." Pressing VITO for specifics at this stage is usually a bad idea. Similarly, you should never try to make VITO "understand" something you think has been missed at this stage of your relationship.

Many salespeople ask me questions that miss this fundamental point. They ask, "How do I make VITO *understand* that he's overlooked an important point when he answers this question *without knowing all the facts*?" You don't! You can't! If you attempt to do so, you will be robbing VITO of ego, power, control, and authority, and your Equal Business Stature will be gone forever!

The key is to put things in VITO's language and work from there.

If you have an opportunity that VITO feels is legitimate, you will get results. If you don't, you won't. Period.

Let me tell a little story that illustrates my point. Many years ago I was working to sell a large computer system to a company, and I had the president come in for a demonstration. My systems engineer, my manager and I were there, giving a demonstration to the president of this company on a relational database. Now, relational databases are very complex animals, and if you're not familiar with them already, I hope you'll forgive me if I don't try to explain them to you here. This president was sitting there, shoulder to shoulder with my systems engineer; the demo started; the systems engineer launched into his explanation; and as he went on, I saw VITO get more and more confused about exactly what was taking place. How could I tell? He got more and more quiet! He stopped asking questions about twenty minutes into the demonstration.

Well, the systems engineer's fingers were flying across the keyboard. He was chattering away, expounding upon all the features of this relational database. We reached a point where the systems engineer had to take a deep breath before diving into another ocean of technical information. During that brief pause, VITO looked at me and asked, "Tony, how much memory does this machine have?"

I think he asked me that because it was the only question he felt comfortable posing—and notice that he didn't pose it to the systems engineer, but to me! Now, my manager (who thought everything was going great) expected me to answer VITO in a certain way. And the systems engineer (who was happy to have a chance to show off all he knew) also expected me to answer VITO in a certain way. What they both expected was for me to say something like, "VITO, this machine has two megabytes of main memory, expandable to eight. And then we could put on an accelerator, which would add another two megabytes, and even that doesn't include the on-line storage, which goes up to three gigabytes." But I didn't say that.

What I said was, "VITO, this machine will never forget anything you tell it."

When I said that, the president started to smile. Then he said, "Finally—something I can understand!"

The systems engineer's eyeballs rolled back in his head. My manager's ears issued forth with clouds of steam. At the end of the presentation, the president shook everyone's hand and went home. My manager called me into the office and said, "Tony, this is a technology-driven organization. When you are asked a question by the president of a company, I expect you to give a proper answer. Don't be so cute. Next time, give the proper technical response to a question like that."

A few months later, when I'd sold that system, I went to my manager's office, slid the $265,000 purchase order right on the desk, and said, "This is for the machine that never forgets."

Whenever you feel the temptation to get VITO to understand, stop—unless you want to see how VITOs act when they feel insecure. (And you'll never want to see that more than once in a lifetime.) Knowledge is power, and VITOs, as a rule, don't like to be in any situation in which they feel they know less than the other people in the room.

It's a funny thing about salespeople. Our first instinct is to talk change, change, change, to our customers. That's a brick wall! VITOs know they know their business better than you do. When you tell them they have to change, or that they don't understand—you lose big time.

So what *do* you say? Let's assume you get a less than iron-sure "no" at this point to your "would-you-buy-from-us" question, a "no" that sounds like it might have a little daylight around the edges. Try something like this.

> *You:* Mr. Benefito, your advice is important to me. If the president of a company that was *your* best prospective customer said no at this point to one of your best salespeople, what would you expect your person to do?

That's the technique that works best for me, and I strongly suggest that you use it. But if you—or, perhaps, your sales manager—feel you must, despite my warnings, ask about the *why* behind VITO's objection, try this approach.

> *You:* Mr. Benefito, you obviously have good reasons for saying no at this point. Would you please share them with me?

If there is daylight in the sale, you will know it after using one of these two approaches.

Four Rules

There are four cardinal rules for dealing with VITO early on. They are:

1. Be specific.
2. Use time-lines.
3. Always deliver what you promise.
4. Never challenge VITO's ego, power, control, and authority.

Things are likely to get pretty hectic in a meeting with VITO; you may have difficulty taking down notes or remembering where you are in the cycle. Here is my promise to you, though: If you remember the four rules I've just outlined for you, none of that will matter.

Where Do You Go from Here?

We've now covered the basic outline of your initial contact with VITO, whether that contact takes place in person, on the phone, or a combination of the two. In the next chapter, you'll find advice on the best ways to involve VITO in the sales cycle as it progresses.

Chapter Fifteen:
Keeping VITO Involved

Let's assume you receive positive feedback from VITO after asking your initial questions, but have been told in no uncertain terms that you must deal with Seymour. This is not an uncommon result, and it's nothing to get discouraged about. The message you're getting is a simple one: VITO is a prudent business person who values the opinions of the people in the organization. That's fine. Your objective is simply to *involve VITO in the process from the beginning and be in a position to broadcast your findings to VITO throughout the entire cycle.*

Warning! The tactics we'll be examining in this chapter will not, repeat, *not* work with municipalities, government agencies, or similar groups. When government bodies buy something, they go out to bid; when the bids are sent out, the doors are closed. Period. You cannot get in to see these people; in fact, you will probably be breaking the law if you try to do so. Other vendors can file complaints if you try to meet with people making purchasing decisions after the bids are opened. In such instances, you will, alas, be unable to bring VITO—or anyone else— to the plate as your ally in the same way you would be able to (and with perfect confidence in your propriety) in other settings.

Keeping VITO Appraised

Within two or three days of your first meeting with your feature-hungry friend Seymour, which I'll assume you need no coaching on, call VITO. Ask if you can drop by alone to chat briefly and provide an executive briefing on your meeting with Seymour. You should probably specify that the meeting will last less than, say, five minutes. VITO probably won't have patience for anything much longer.

If you have followed the steps outlined in the previous chapter, correctly identifying VITO's mindset and asking appropriate questions, VITO should agree to meet briefly with you. After all, you've got Equal Business Stature!

While in VITO's office, incorporate something like the following into your conversation:

> *You:* Looks like Seymour and I will be spending a lot of time together pursuing some ideas for your organization. Could you do me one personal favor? When the decision is made for or against my company, would you grant me the honor of an in-person visit with you?

If VITO agrees, make a note of the date of your request and put it in your prospect file.

If VITO rejects your request for a meeting, say:

> *You:* VITO, my company will be spending some pretty significant time and resources over the next (several months). Meeting your criteria is of the utmost importance to us. If we fail to earn your business, my company has to continue to learn.

My own experience is that, if the work leading up to this point has been done properly, VITO will almost always agree to your request for a meeting when you frame it in these terms. Good thing, too, since this promise for a meeting is of the utmost importance in your later management of the sales cycle. (In the unlikely event that you cannot win an agreement for a later meeting, your only option in the event of trouble will be the Pigeonhole Recovery Letter described in an earlier chapter.)

Loss Recovery

If, at any point during the sales cycle, you detect any signals that you're losing, call VITO for the face-to-face meeting.

> *You:* Mr. Benefito, back on (exact date when VITO promised you a meeting), you promised me the privilege of an in-person visit, whether your decision was for or against my solution. Will you honor your promise and grant me that visit tomorrow?
>
> *VITO:* Guess I did promise you. Come on in at 10:15.

If you've done your job correctly up to this point, which includes keeping in touch with VITO throughout the sales cycle, you should have no trouble getting a positive response of some kind to your request.

Don't get nervous about setting this appointment. (In fact, nervousness in asking for it is probably a bigger obstacle than anything VITO has to offer.) VITO is, as a general rule, quite honest—perhaps the most honest person in the organization—and will keep promises. You should not have to work too hard to win your hearing.

You must now get your manager involved in the sale—or perhaps another person of higher rank in your organization. For our purposes, we'll refer to this person as "your manager" here.

Prepare your manager to assist you with this meeting, your last chance to win this account. If possible, prepare a compelling visual presentation of your solution. *Keep it simple.* Don't deal in abstracts or intangibles—find something concrete, something hard or soft or hot or cold or wet or dry that VITO can hold. Then, with your manager, isolate your best success stories and endorsements, and stand back and let the Guiding VITO Principle come into play.

What, you may ask, is the Guiding VITO Principle? It's a simple idea that underlies everything we've covered so far.

> You can't sell VITO. Only VITO can sell VITO.

What's more, VITOs *love to convince themselves that they've made the right decision.* Let this predilection of theirs work in your favor.

Don't press. Don't panic. Don't shower VITO with a blizzard of supporting documentation—that's Seymour stuff. Spotlight your successes, make it tangible, make it *stick* . . . then stand back. If there are silences, *wait them out* and hear what VITO has to say.

If this final attempt fails, at least you got a last shot. And as you leave VITO's office, you'll hear your manager say, "You did the best you could; that wasn't the right deal for us." Even if it doesn't come down your way, you'll be a hero in your manager's eyes.

Win Broadcasting

As the sales cycle matures, you may see clear signals that you're winning. Now is the time to broadcast this very likely possibility. This is the time for a trial commitment to opening a business relationship with VITO. Remember, you are not "closing a sale!" (To my way of thinking, the only way you "close" a sale is to lose it.)

Follow the same principles outlined above in securing a meeting with VITO. When you sit down with VITO, outline all the progress you've made with Seymour.

Make Seymour a hero in VITO's eyes. You'll have everybody smiling, and you will have laid the groundwork for a long-term partnership.

Show VITO all the potential savings you and Seymour have identified together. Quantify everything. Speak openly and specifically. Do not equivocate. Blow your own horn and be straightforward in the results you foresee delivering to VITO's organization.

At some point in the meeting, say something like this:

> *You:* Mr. Benefito, as you know, we're absolutely committed to developing a long-term partnership that benefits your organization. When my competition—(and here mention all the competitors you know have been calling on this account)—when these folks find out that you're favoring our solution, they may come in here and try to pull a few fast moves. Are you going to be able to resist them and those tempting "special deals" they're going to show you? Are you going to be able to resist their sly little "special offers"? Will you say "no" to them?

Now you must watch VITO's body language with a very critical eye. Your "sure order" may be in serious trouble, even at this late stage.

At the conclusion of your meeting, strive to leave the door open for a return visit. *Never, under any circumstances, leave your VITO alone during the last few critical weeks of the sales cycle.* If you can't arrange a meeting, call!

Once again, if you manage the endgame correctly, you won't have to worry about "closing." (And isn't *that* a relief.) During your Win

Broadcast meeting, VITO will in all likelihood *tell* you when to start and what to do next. That's exactly where you want to be.

Chapter Sixteen:
Success!

You got the "yes"! Congratulations. You've developed a business relationship with VITO's organization. You've opened a new door and established a new partnership.

As I have reminded you throughout this book, you must not imagine that you can "close" a sale with VITO and then walk away.

You must personally see that the results you promised are delivered. You must maintain contact with VITO and with all other important decision makers in the organization *throughout the lifecycle of the account.* In this chapter you'll find some ideas on how to do that.

Formalize the Partnership

Look around the American business landscape today. Which companies are in trouble? The companies that

- got complacent.
- took customers for granted.
- read their own PR materials and believed them.
- thought the words "market share" were some kind of magic incantation that would ward off customer-focused competitors.
- depended too much on high-priced marketing plans.

All those companies are dead or dying. The companies that are going through the roof are the ones that are committing to becoming partners for life with their customers. Show VITO which category your firm falls into.

After the bottom line is signed and the widget delivery is scheduled, if you have not already done so, prepare a blank binder with your company logo on the front. Either schedule a formal "good-to-be-working-with-you" meeting with VITO—or, if this doesn't work out, briefly pop into VITO's office while you are visiting with someone else and hand the binder over. As we outlined earlier, VITO will probably say something like, "What's this? It's empty." And you'll say, "It won't be for long. You'll be getting progress reports from me by mail at least (every month)." Then you update VITO with success stories, written in the same concise, results-oriented style you used in your initial letter. (If you have already presented VITO with this binder, use the "good-to-be-working-with-you" meeting to drop off a brief summary of your goals for the project.)

Be sure all the letters you pass along to VITO are three-hole punched, so that they fit in the binder. Every time your product or service keeps a disaster from happening, saves money, or results in a more efficient workforce, you send another memo in VITO-speak. Where do you get the information? From Seymour! At first, you can put together a simple questionnaire about your service. Ask Seymour to do "a quick analysis." (Seymour *loves* to do analyses!) Then make a point of scheduling regular meetings so you can keep tabs on all the wonderful successes Seymour is implementing . . . with your help.

This is not an exercise in creative writing, or an effort to show VITO how well you work with Seymour. You must focus on results. You must anchor your benefit in VITO's consciousness, and you must do it on a regular basis. That's what your new partnership is all about. Be unlike every other salesperson VITO runs into. Make sure VITO gets the message from the front line. Take the time and trouble. Send the memos.

Take Advantage of the Fact that VITO Knows You're a Damned Good Businessperson

Let's be honest. You've done a hell of a job here, and VITO knows it.

Inevitably, VITO will say something good about you during an in-person meeting. Right then, at that very moment, write the comment down on your notepad. Put quote marks around it, hand it back to VITO, and say, "VITO, would you mind personalizing this for me?" VITO will say something like, "What for?" Show VITO a copy of the same benefit letter you initially sent. Then say, "I want to include that quote in a letter that's going out next week to fifty (manufacturers) in (Chicago)." (Of course, you should never be so foolish as to ask permission to use VITO's words to sell to a direct competitor.) Be ready to give VITO a list of companies you'll be sending the letter to.

Nine times out of ten, VITO will agree to your suggestion. *Ten* times out of ten, VITO will wish there were more salespeople like you working for VITO, Incorporated.

You may worry that a move like this will seem presumptuous on your part. Well, it might with Seymour. It won't with VITO. In VITO's eyes, you can only *earn* points by being a good businessperson.

As you leave your "good-to-be-working-with-you" meeting, ask, "VITO, is there anyone *that you would like to introduce me to* that I might be able to help in a similar or even greater way?" (Note that you don't say "anyone that I could call . . . ." That's too self-centered.) Get ready to take down the highest-quality category of referrals a salesperson can get.

"Yeah," VITO will say, "Jane Smith over at ABC might be a good person to call." Write down the information. But don't stop there! Ask, "VITO, what's Jane Smith's secretary's name?" VITO will smile and say, "Jamie." Return the smile and say thank you. Shake hands. Leave.

VITO just did your prospecting work for you. Make a beeline for your word processor; draft a letter for this new VITO. This type of referral represents the only time that you should adapt or adjust the formula for your postscript. When VITO identifies a prospect for you in this way, add a sentence to the beginning of the Action P.S.: "VITO Benefito of VITO, Incorporated suggested that I give you a call . . . ." Jamie will see VITO's name in the headline and Action P.S., and will more than likely recognize that name. You're in!

No, you don't have to worry about getting referrals to Seymours from VITOs. My experience has been that VITOs refer VITOs, and nobody but. And those referrals carry weight!

Personalize

I've already spoken briefly about the danger of loading VITOs down with technical drawings, manuals, schematics, or other Seymour-friendly communications. Instead, leave your "good-to-be-working-with-you" meeting with VITO with a color picture of your company's smiling staff, gathered in front of the headquarters building. Make it abundantly clear that VITO has signed on with a group of *businesspeople* who are committed to delivering results.

If you must leave something in the way of written material, keep it brief (one page is best) and make sure it's in color. I've found that color pie-charts work especially well. VITOs are bored by black and white.

Do What You've Promised—and Stay Tuned

When VITOs go places, they take along the people who helped them. That means that, if you make absolutely certain you deliver the goods, you may well get a call two years from now—when VITO leaves to take an even bigger job at an even bigger company! This sort of thing happens to me all the time. One of my very biggest accounts came from a call that took place in just this way!

Chapter Seventeen:
Some Final Thoughts on Your Current Accounts

Now that you are familiar with the fundamentals of the Selling to VITO system, I want to share some final thoughts on dealing with Seymours. Specifically, I want to look at the problems you face, not in new accounts where VITO is the initial contact, but in existing accounts where you may currently be dealing with a Seymour as your sole contact.

You may remember that, at the outset of this book, I urged you to take another look at your existing accounts, and to make an effort to meet the VITOs in your current customer base. As we move toward the final portion of the program, I'd like to take this opportunity to remind you of the importance of doing this—and to caution you against complacency when it comes to dealing with accounts you've "already sold."

Implementing the advice I'm offering on this score may be among the most difficult things for you to follow through on. I know, because I've been there.

I realize that, once you get the commission check, you don't want to "mess with a winning formula." And I can certainly acknowledge that it's tough—initially—to talk yourself into going to a "closed" account and asking to talk to the top person. But it is nevertheless essential to your long-term success as a salesperson. You must move beyond Seymour, even in your current accounts.

"Come on, Tony, a Sale Is a Sale. Why Make Such a Big Deal about This?"

Because a sale is temporary. A partnership is long-term.

Some sales are essentially matters of short-term mutual convenience. Some sales are long-term partnerships. In today's business environment, if you confuse the former with the latter, *you lose*.

Why should you take the trouble to "VITO-proof" your current customers? Because it's a heck of a lot more expensive—both for you and for your company—to find new customers than it is to hold on to and develop existing ones. And when I say "develop," I'm talking about expanding your partnership to include add-ons as well as completely new solutions to problems in the organization.

In the long run, VITO is either going to be your ally and business partner or your enemy—the one who makes things happen for you in the organization, or the one who scans the printout, sees something that looks vaguely like the "fat" the accountants have been whining about, has to make a decision, and cuts you off. (An even more frightening scenario, of course, is the one in which VITO doesn't know you exist—and cuts you off when your competition makes one of those "special offers.") You are going to run into VITO one way or the other. It's better on your terms. Believe me; this is experience speaking.

"But I Sold Seymour on the Bells and Whistles!"

I hear something like this at just about every seminar I do. "Tony, you said earlier that VITOs like benefits, and Seymours like features. Well, I closed this sale by pointing Seymour toward all the fancy new gizmos and whatnots and double-insulated thingamabobs. VITO doesn't care about those! What's more, VITO's going to *ask* me how those bells and whistles translate into benefits—and I don't know!"

Find out. Or, if you prefer not to, don't be surprised when you lose the account.

It really is that simple. If you've sold things to Seymour based on a feature set, and no one, including you, has made the business argument to VITO or, at the very least, VITO's close friend the manager, about the benefit to the organization, you are exposed on a critical front. Your long-term relationship is in jeopardy.

When the competition shows up on your customer's doorstep and offers a brighter gizmo, a bigger whatnot, a triple-insulated thingamabob, guess what? You're history—in less time than it takes to say "Seymour!" And that's just the most likely scenario. When the competition shows up on *VITO's* doorstep and makes a compelling case for a new widget that will actually deliver a tangible benefit to VITO's organization, you're history in less time than it takes to say *"I should have listened to Tony."*

Yes, VITO has the ultimate veto power. If VITO doesn't understand the value of what you have to offer, even some rinkydink company with some rinkydink product or service can knock you out. Why take the risk? Because it's simpler to do nothing? Maybe so. After all, when you come right down to it, it's simplicity itself to lose an account—and, for that matter, your job! It's the consequences that are so difficult.

Where to Start

Many salespeople avoid the steps I'm suggesting in this chapter because they are intimidated by the thought of approaching VITOs at the most tenuous accounts on their list. Don't worry about those accounts at first. Start with the ones you know you're delivering results for.

Pick out the nicest, happiest, most approachable Seymour you know, the one who works for a company that is absolutely ecstatic about what you do. (Later, of course, you'll adapt what follows so that you can work your way through your entire customer list—or, at any rate, the ones you want to keep for a while.)

At one of your many meetings with Seymour, say, "Seymour, your company is one of my best customers. My president/sales manager/regional vice president (align the title to the size of the account) has personally asked me to identify ten of my top clients, and I've identified you as one of those. I've been asked to set up a meeting between me, you and your president, Ms. Benefito, to thank both of you for the value of our relationship."

In some cases, Seymour will agree to arrange the meeting for you without giving you any static at all. (This is particularly likely when you are dealing with an account to which you are delivering solid results, and Seymour wants VITO to know it.) In other cases, Seymour will ask, "What's up? Why do you want to meet with her all of a sudden?"

If Seymour asks this, whip out a long, official-looking list. Yes, the list must be on paper. Remember, Seymours love substantiating documentation. This list of yours should take up one or two full pages, and it should be printed on your organization's official stationery. It should be signed by *your* company's VITO. (Here we have yet another example of the *right* way to use your organization's logo and identifying materials, which do indeed play an important role in your sales work.)

Then you say something like this.

You: Seymour, my president has told me to get Ms. Benefito's valued opinion on the questions outlined in this memo. I'm supposed to go over all of this. It would be great if you would come along with me—but if you don't, my marching orders are to get a meeting with Ms. Benefito, ask her these questions, and shake her hand. You know how it is when you get an order from the top, right?

The "if-you-don't-want-to-go-with-me" part is important. Your objective is not necessarily to get Seymour to *arrange* the meeting for you, but to at least *let Seymour know what is going to take place.* In larger companies, it's a good bet that your Seymour has never even met VITO, so asking for help in setting up a meeting is not the way to go. Take the initiative for contacting VITO yourself, but let your contact at the company know exactly what you're doing.

You're probably wondering: What is on that long, official-looking list? *It doesn't matter*—as long as the questions you and your superior select meet five important criteria.

ONE: There must be a lot of them.

TWO: The questions must be ones Seymour cannot answer.

THREE: The questions must cover issues that you can talk about with VITO.

FOUR: The issues you address must reference VITO's annual report or mission statement.

FIVE: The questions must cover issues in which Seymour has no interest whatsoever, and on which Seymour has no opinions whatsoever.

Examples of the types of questions you might decide to include on your list appear below.

- "What are Ms. Benefito's revenue growth plans for (year)?"
- "What are Ms. Benefito's expense reduction plans for (year)?"
- "What are Ms. Benefito's ideas for increasing quality control for (year)?"

- "What are Ms. Benefito's primary strategic goals in expanding into the (Pacific Southwest) market?"

- "How do institutional sales fit into Ms. Benefito's growth plan for (year)?"

- "What dangers does Ms. Benefito foresee in extending financing to health-care organizations considering the transitional phase the nation now finds itself in with regard to payment mechanisms?"

- "How does Ms. Benefito plan to address the growing industry trend of high turnover among upper-level executives?"

- "What marketing initiatives will Ms. Benefito consider during the critical first year of the (King Funds) project?"

- "How does Ms. Benefito plan to attract, develop, and retain talented mid-level employees in (year)?"

- "What expansion of product lines and services to clients does Ms. Benefito anticipate in (year)?"

- "How does Ms. Benefito plan to reduce average cost-of-sale figures in the (Northeast region) in (year)?"

- "What must we do to continue to meet your criteria as a true business partner?"

- "What are Ms. Benefito's plans for (division of the company Seymour has no responsibility for)?"

That last question is a particularly good one to set up. If your Seymour is in engineering, pose a question about accounting. If your Seymour is in accounting, pose a question about marketing.

If you're still uncertain about the kinds of questions you and your superior should put on this list, go back to chapter four. You'll find ideas there on things VITOs like to talk about.

"What if Seymour Says I Have to Meet Someone Else First?"

Do it. Work your way up the chain. Present the same list and the same situation to the next person in line. Explain what you've been asked to do by your VITO: get into the president's office, ask a few brief questions, and shake hands. Be firm. Be polite. Be professional. Show your unshakable confidence. You'll build loyalty and start a groundswell. Remember, you're one of the good guys: You're *already* working with this company to solve problems.

"What if Seymour Says It's Impossible for Me to Get a Meeting with VITO under Any Circumstances?"

Call Seymour's bluff. Say, "Seymour, can you please call my boss and tell her I can't go?" Seymour will usually back down.

If Seymour doesn't, there's a good chance you're dealing with a status issue. Ask your sales manager to try to arrange the meeting with VITO. If this effort is successful (and it usually is), your sales manager has an easy job to perform at the end of the meeting: to ask VITO, "Well, Ms. Benefito, I just have one more question—would you like to meet the sales rep who's been parking in your parking lot and drinking out of your water fountain for the last few months?" Usually, VITO will say something like, "Sure, why not. Let's set up a time." You may then call Seymour and say, "Seymour, you're not going to believe this. The meeting went really well, so thanks for helping me prepare my manager and everything, but guess what? VITO wants to meet with me. Do you want to meet with me or shall I go alone?"

This is a nonthreatening scenario for Seymour, and it's an extremely effective tactic for getting you in the door to meet with VITO.

"So What Happens at This Meeting?"

During this meeting, you will simply review your successes with VITO, provide hard information on the benefits you and Seymour have been able to deliver. Show off plenty of color pie-charts that show quantifiable, measurable results. Most important, *listen and take notes* as VITO outlines plans for the future in response to your questions. Of course, you shouldn't feel obligated to pepper VITO with every single one of the questions on your list; ask broad questions that encompass all the key points. In the end, the only questions that really matter are the ones you would pose during your initial call to a new VITO.

At the meeting's conclusion, you can adapt two of the techniques we've already discussed: the coffee cup or other small gift with the benefit tag, and the binder for success stories. The difference, for the purpose of this visit, is that with these VITOs, you *already have* successes to attach to these two gifts. Isolate the most impressive success on the tag you attach to the coffee cup. Include two or three informal but compelling success stories in the binder when you give it to VITO. (If, for some strange reason, you are not able to attend this meeting, but your sales manager or some other superior is, they should pass along these gifts for you.)

Pick Ten Customers to Target Right Now

Are you ready for a surprise? The meetings will be fun!

Try it. Stop right now and write it down and put it on your calendar. "I want to meet with the VITO of ABC, Inc. next Monday." Then make it happen!

By the way, if you're working with a contact who's at the Manager level, the same technique applies. Go to your contact and say, "You know what? We've been doing business together for (five years). My president asked me if I'd met with your president eyeball-to-eyeball yet, and I had to say no. Then he asked me to set up a meeting." You may not even have to show these folks a list; they're much less intimidated by VITOs than Seymours are. Managers are more likely to say, "Sure, let's head up to VITO's office right now."

A Brief Story for Your Further Edification

A long time ago, before I developed this system, I paid a visit to an account of mine.

This was during my time at Hewlett-Packard. I was doing what a good salesperson was supposed to do. I was getting out there and shaking hands. I was talking to Seymour, reminding him of how wonderful our technology and systems were and how our future systems would be even more powerful.

As I was sitting and chatting with Seymour, I happened to notice a little blue box on his bookshelf. The box had three white letters on the spine: IBM.

I said, "Seymour, what's that up there?"

Seymour laughed and said, "Oh, that's just a demo the production department wants to look at." I smiled and nodded. We continued our conversation.

If I'd known then what I know now, I would have been in a position to contact VITO and demonstrate exactly what my system and company could do, how it could continue to deliver the best results for his organization's specific applications. But I didn't do that. Because I was a "good salesperson" who followed the rules, I knew that Mr. Benefito didn't need to waste his time talking to me. Who was I to talk out of turn, anyway? And why would I want to jeopardize my relationship with Seymour?

During another visit to Seymour's office, I saw three of those little boxes. A few months later, I made my "please-don't-drop-us" presentation to Seymour, when it turned out those little blue boxes had been multiplying at an alarming rate. And just under four months after I had first noticed that first little box on Seymour's bookshelf, I was informed that Mr. Benefito had personally decided to change over to IBM. VITO's company *donated* the system I had sold Seymour to a college in my territory!

Ouch.

Chapter Eighteen:
Some Common Questions

In this chapter, we'll take a look at some of the most common questions that come up during my seminars. (By the way, if you have questions of your own, or any suggestions whatsoever regarding my program, please feel free to contact me. Use the questionnaire that appears in Appendix C, near the end of the book.)

I'm still a little confused about how to categorize some of my contacts. Some people seem to me to be both Managers and Seymours!

With the right-sizing movement in full swing, there is a fascinating phenomenon whereby managers are expected to have a solid command of the technical aspects of the company's needs for products and services, and must at times play the role of Seymours. If you run into a situation like this, just remember the basic principle. Only VITO gets to wear any hat at all in the organization.

It was scary at first, but I tried asking VITO for leads as you suggested. It really worked! The only question I have is this: What do I do with the leads that VITO gives me that seem inappropriate for my business? They must be good for something.

Call them anyway! Sometimes opportunity waits in the strangest places. Remember, lots of VITOs serve as board members of other companies that may need what you have to offer. Never give away or throw away a VITO referral until you yourself have checked it out and exhausted all possibilities.

■　　■　　■

I'm being stonewalled! What do I do when I've been given a memo informing me that it's official company policy to stay with a certain vendor. The VITO is in the "home office"—in Europe! What do I do?

"Tony, we *have* to buy XYZ—I've got a memo from the head office to work with that vendor only. Look. It's signed by VITO himself." That's the kind of talk I was facing during the dark days when I was competing with "industry standards." I turned any number of those accounts around, and you can too—by tracking down the person with profit-and-loss responsibility for the area you're trying to sell to.

So you can't get VITO to give you an in-person meeting. So what? The vast majority of business today is conducted by phone, fax, or modem anyway. (And I hear tell that there is actually telephone software available now that provides a real-time translation between callers who don't speak each other's languages.) Obviously, my first preference would be for you to meet with VITOs in person, but when that's impossible, there's no reason for your sales to suffer. A good, solid letter or fax followed up by a phone call can and will work wonders.

Follow VITO across the county, across the state, and across the country if necessary. And don't be intimidated. Stand your ground, make your case, and, when appropriate, ask VITO how much the loyalty is costing.

One important caveat is in order here: If you are trying to do business with VITOs from other cultures, you will have to adapt your techniques to your VITO's background. Obviously, space limitations prohibit me from exploring this complicated topic in detail, but suffice to say that what is appreciated as an aggressive, no-nonsense style by an American executive may be perceived as incomprehensible rudeness by a VITO of another culture. *Do not* try to use the techniques in this book to sell to a VITO from another culture before discussing the changes you will need to make with an experienced business professional who has worked in that culture.

I still feel a little queasy about calling VITO directly, rather than having someone of comparable stature at my organization initiate the contact. Any thoughts?

We've covered this in detail already, but the issue is worth examining once again—and with a slightly different spin—because *fear* is one of the primary reasons salespeople are slow to implement the ideas between these covers.

Some people listen to what I have to say, think, "Hey, that's a good idea, that might actually work if I ever got up the nerve to try it," then do *absolutely nothing*—because someone, somewhere along the line told them that all business contacts have to be "like to like," with sales reps talking to data processing coordinators, regional vice presidents talking to regional vice presidents, and so on.

Don't let that happen to you.

Think of it this way: If only VITOs could call up other VITOs, nothing would ever happen! Henry Ford would probably never have secured the support he needed to build the Model T automobile. Bill Gates would never have made that fateful deal with IBM that sent his company, Microsoft, into the stratosphere. And, perhaps closest to home as far as this writer is concerned, I never would have hit my quota at Hewlett-Packard or built a successful sales training organization!

It does not have to be like to like. You can call anyone you want. It's a free country. (And it's a *really* free country for those who can establish Equal Business Stature with VITO.)

Again, this is not theory. This is what I put into practice myself, day after day. I have personally contacted Ted Turner and Donald Trump. I've called the presidents of multi-billion-dollar companies. I've called public officials, private officials, in-between officials, you name it. The title on my business card is not CEO—it's businessperson! My motto is, if the mayor's making the decision, *I write a letter to the mayor and then follow up with a call.* If "everything's all set" and "the decision's already been made, it just has to be rubber stamped," *I find the person with the rubber stamp.* No kidding. All you have to do to see the wisdom of this approach is to try it a few times.

That's right, just try it—if only to prove me wrong. If it gives you the willies to say to yourself that this is the way you'll be doing things from now on, then just follow my advice with 100 new VITO prospects, exactly as I've described it. You'll be so impressed with the results that all the fear will melt away . . . and you'll be surprised you ever hesitated. You won't want to go back. I didn't.

If I hook up with the Chief Financial Officer, does that person count as a VITO?

Maybe not. Odds are that you're looking at a very high-ranking Manager.

As a general rule, those who manage financial and accounting functions are not the most important players in the corporate decision-making process. That applies even when the person in question has an upscale title. Of course, there are exceptions, but they tend to be few and far between.

The CFO may be an important ally in the organization, but chances are he or she is not the VITO to whom you should be targeting your letter and follow-up call. Don't put all your eggs in this person's basket.

If you're ever in contact with someone you have been led to believe is a VITO, but whom you are unable to classify confidently in your own mind, try this. At the end of your presentation before the group, close your briefcase, look the person you think might be VITO straight in the eye, and say, "VITO, are you prepared to move forward? Are you prepared to begin to use our solution and realize the kinds of benefits we've been talking about?"

Let's say you get an answer along these lines: "This sounds very interesting, but I need to discuss it with people. Why don't you call me back in thirty days." At that point you can either wait the thirty days, or you can use what I call the "VITO Wannabe Flush."

Here's how it works. You say, "VITO, if you didn't have thirty days—and I know that you do—but if you had to make the decision right now, what would it be?" That takes guts! But it will tell you something very important about the person you're dealing with.

If this person is really a VITO, you will get an answer—something like, "Well, I don't have to, but if I did, I'd have to say that right now I'd stay with the current vendor." Or, "If I had to make up my mind right now, I'd do business with your company, because I honestly like what I've seen so far."

VITOS *will* answer that question for two reasons. Number one, they can. Number two, they won't hedge on a direct challenge like this before members of their own organization.

But if you hear, "I'm not prepared to answer that right now," or any variation on it, guess what? You're talking to a VITO wannabe, not a VITO.

How do you contact VITO if the decision to purchase your product or service is being made by a committee?

Research, persistence, and the ability to pick out the leading member of a group—or the person to whom that group reports. There always is one or the other, and that person is your VITO.

Want to talk about bureaucratic gridlock? My job at Hewlett-Packard was to sell incredibly complicated, incredibly expensive computer systems to colleges and universities! If I'd rolled over every time someone told me that I had to "wait for the committee's decision," I would have been hung out to dry when my sales manager got around to totaling up the results. I called the chairperson of the committee if it seemed appropriate to do so, and if it didn't, I called the dean of the college. Yes, there is a certain amount of judgment involved here, and certainly you are the ultimate authority on your selling environment. But after a while, you will learn to find the opening. The one thing I can guarantee you is that passively waiting for the "board to make its decision" after a single meeting with Seymour is your ticket to mediocrity, disappointing results, and failure.

One word of advice on tracking down VITOs at municipalities or nonprofit organizations: find out who signs the checks. Then find out who *that* person works for and approach that person. (If they're one and the same, there's no doubt you're looking at VITO.)

Should you quantify actual or projected savings for a VITO at a small company in the same way you would for a VITO at a large company?

Not exactly. For large companies, use a percentage. For smaller ones, use dollar amounts.

I've said it before, but it's worth repeating here: Don't exaggerate when dealing with a VITO, no matter the size of the company! You'll lose credibility . . . and sales. If you say, "We reduced operating costs at ABC Company by three percent," you'd better be able to prove that you reduced the costs across the board. If what you mean is that you reduced costs by that much in a particular division, operating group, or line-item, say that. Accuracy is the rule of the day.

And don't think that three-percent savings levels in a division go unnoticed by VITOs. One of my favorite gambits when dealing with VITOs at big organizations is to say something like, "But, of course, that was just a three-percent decrease. For a large operation like this, three percent might not make that much difference." They come right out of the chair.

I felt uncomfortable with the opening sentences you suggested for the first telephone contact with VITO. Are there any variations?

Sure, but they take a little research. Here's one: "Congratulations on being named to the board of (local charity group)," or something along those lines. If you're willing to do the legwork, this kind of opening can go a very long way indeed.

The important thing to bear in mind when talking to VITOs is that they focus on themselves first, on the organization second (although often, the two are fused), and rarely if ever on you. If you can put something together that takes all this into account, you have my blessings if you want to use it as part of your opening statement.

How do you handle unexpected requests for bids?

Usually, I either ignore them or allot a minimal amount of time, work, and effort to them.

Honestly, if you get an unexpected, mailed request for a bid, the odds are that someone other than you has been helping the prospect write the specs. If anything, you may want to use the information to contact VITO directly, but my own experience has been that all you'll be doing is laying the groundwork for the possibility of a future sale. (Of course, there's nothing wrong with that. But there is a question of keeping your expectations realistic.)

Requests for bids are for Seymours, and they are usually sent out after the bulk of someone else's sales work is done. You may have different experiences in your own industry, but my own instinct after a good many years is that this is usually not worth the trouble. I have yet to win a bid that I didn't know about beforehand.

If you're submitting a bid or proposal on a *current* account, one you've spent some time on, one that VITO knows about, then by all means try to get through to VITO and show what you have before you submit it. You'll get a lot further with VITO than you would with Seymour!

What do I do if VITO asks me for the source of my Headline Statement?

No prizes for getting the right answer here. Give the source—and offer to fax it to VITO's office. If you're quoting an annual report, identify it and offer to fax the page. If you're quoting an article, identify it and offer to fax that. If your Benefit Statement quotes someone who gave you information directly, be prepared to provide a telephone number and suggest a time for VITO to call that person.

This question usually comes up when people play fast and loose with the details while developing a Headline Statement. Don't do it. VITO will call you on the carpet every time. And that's not exactly a great way to build Equal Business Stature.

I've tried making the calls the way you describe them. Overall, they went fine, but there sure were a lot of silences. How do I handle those?

Got a silence? Wait it out.

For our purposes, there are only two kinds, and waiting is the right prescription for each. The first is when VITO isn't really paying attention to what you're saying: "No, go ahead Tony, I'm just signing some checks here." I always say, "No, that's okay, I'll wait." And I wait it out. To do anything else is to give up Equal Business Stature at a very early point in the relationship, and you don't want to do that.

The other kind of silence comes when VITO is thinking of how to respond to something you have said or suggested. You *must* wait here, even though it may be uncomfortable to do so, because the conversation and the sales cycle will not progress with a VITO if you talk while your business partner is deciding something. Often we feel an instinct to talk to prove to VITO just how much we know, or to confirm to ourselves that progress really is taking place; usually, we prove only the opposite in each case. Let VITO drive the conversation; no matter how uncomfortable the silences may feel, wait them out.

*I tried the "please define price" tactic you suggested, and I
bombed. I lost VITO to a firm that was offering a similar system
for $10,000 less. Any other ideas on overcoming a price hurdle?*

The problem may have been that VITO saw the two systems as
identical. Were they really?

In most situations of this kind, the two packages being compared
are not the same at all. Your job is to find everything that you offer that
the competition does not, and quantify the impact of each one of
these to VITO's organization. Perhaps it's training. Perhaps it's follow-
up. Perhaps it's higher quality or a lower reject rate. Whatever it is,
your job in this situation is to quantify it and present it in terms that
VITO can appreciate.

*During an initial phone call with a VITO, I asked the big
questions I was supposed to—and got shot down on all of them.
What do you do in a situation like that?*

This one's really pretty simple. Rather than coming up with three
more questions about where VITO wants the widget department to go
over the next quarter, just ask, "Well, if these are not important to you
right now, what *are* you focusing your attention on until the end of the
(quarter)?" If you get a positive response, follow VITO's lead. If you
don't, and if you feel there's no way for you to do business with this
VITO, say thank you and try someone else.

*I got through to VITO, made an appointment, had a great
visit—and then got stuck with Seymour again, because that's who
VITO said I should talk to. The Pigeonhole Recovery Letter might
work, but you said that was for a different scenario—when I had
not yet met with VITO—and anyway, I'd rather not bring my
manager in so often. Any ideas on how I can get out of this?*

In addition to the ideas on win broadcast and loss recovery, there
are a few additional techniques you can use to get Seymour pulling on
the right end of the rope. First, play to existing predispositions. Start the
sales cycle from the get-go, just as you would if you had not contacted
VITO, and show off all the documentation, all the spec sheets, and all
the double-insulated thingamabobs. Win Seymour as an ally. Make it
clear that your objective is to turn Seymour into a hero in VITO's eyes.

If you sense that you are being met with resistance at any point in the sales cycle, say something like this: "You know, a couple of weeks ago when I (met/spoke) with VITO, she said that you were really busy, that you had a lot on your plate—but that this was so important that we should get together and spend some time on it." This will usually get things moving again.

More static? During an in-person visit, say, "Seymour, I'm in a funny position here. I promised VITO I would help in (one month/two months/three months, or whatever the time-frame you discussed with VITO was). Could you call VITO right now while I'm here?" If even *this* does not clear your way, either you or your manager should call VITO to bring the roadblock to VITO's attention. You should always *ask* VITO what steps to take next. "VITO, how do you want me to proceed with this?"*

The VITO I called agreed to meet with me—but when I showed up he chewed me out about some problem he had with our company five years ago, before I even got here. How do you respond to something like that?

If the root causes of the problem VITO has brought to your attention are still in place, then you can't. Shake hands, say goodbye, and outline the problem to your sales manager once you make it back to the office. But in the likelier event that your company has changed things (even if the change is ever so slight), you can adapt one of the lines we looked at earlier.

> *You:* VITO, I have to ask your advice. If you had this problem in *your* organization, how would you handle it?

---

* When, after a good first call with VITO, you are sent along to Seymour, I suggest that you avoid, at least initially, mentioning that VITO was the one who suggested you talk to Seymour. Why? You don't yet know how Seymour sees VITO! There may even be resentment on Seymour's part for anything VITO sends along. Mention this endorsement only later on, if at all. Appealing to VITO's suggestion that you talk to Seymour is a tactic to be used when you are looking at a logjam and can see no other way to break it up.

This may well bring about a brief respite in the shelling. Of course, if VITO tells you what is going to be necessary for you to win back the business, you must take it all down on paper and promise to report back on a specific date. If the attack continues, however, you might make one last attempt to salvage the situation by saying something like this:

> *You:* Well, Mr. Benefito, we didn't do all those things, but we did do some of them. The fact is, we have a better president now and so I'm back on your doorstep. We are helping some companies and I honestly don't know whether or not we can help you, but the only way we can go forward is if you tell me the next step for us to take.

I've got a VITO I really want to sell. I followed your advice, sent all the letters and faxes, did all the follow-up calls—and still can't get through. What do I do now?

For particularly tough VITOs, I suggest you get your company to make the minimal investment required to put together a sharp audio-tape, complete with honest-to-goodness fellow VITOs—or perhaps your own organization's VITO—praising your problem-solving solutions at the outset. (You may, if you wish, record these testimonials with a handheld recorder, then have them edited in. It will add a sense of realism!) In essence, you are assembling an audio contact letter that VITO can pop into the tape player on the drive home. By the way, if you keep the basic tracks, you can update this tape for other VITOs at minimal cost.

The last thing on the tape should be your Action P.S.: "Mr. Bene-fito, I'm going to wait three days so you have the chance to listen to this; then I'll be calling you at 8:00 on Wednesday morning. If I've picked a bad time to call, please have Leslie call me so we can set up a more convenient one."

Put the tape in a modest, professional-looking package, then follow up.

Chapter Nineteen:
Congratulations!

You've made it. That's the end of the program.

If I had to pick out one piece of advice to leave you with, it would be that you appreciate, as I have come to, the value of a single word. This is a word so important that it will affect your relationship with *everyone* you come in contact with, whether it's in a business, family, or social setting. It's a word that will allow you to take a quantum leap in every aspect of your life.

Some time ago, my wife and I went to a major benefit banquet and had the privilege of being in the V.I.P. reception area. We saw movie stars, pop stars, political figures—our eyes were practically bulging out of our heads. I'd never been in a situation like that: shoulder-to-shoulder with some of the biggest celebrities in the world. I remember thinking that I had, for the first time, an idea of what it's like to be in the presence of royalty.

It was a magical night. At the end of the evening, we were outside the building waiting for our car to be brought around. I glanced at my wife, who was looking especially attractive that evening, and for a moment I thought of saying something like, "Wasn't it an honor to be in that room tonight?" But instead of saying that, I said, "Nancy, it was a real honor to be with *you* this evening."

Her eyes lit up. She said, "You know, we've been married sixteen years, and that's only the second time I've heard you say that word."

"What word?" I asked.

"Honor," she explained. "The first time was when we took our wedding vow, when you said 'love, honor, and cherish.' " She smiled a smile I'll never forget. All that weekend I tried to find ways to show Nancy that I was very much honored to be with her.

On Monday morning, I was still thinking about the word. I remember observing that, in other languages, there are many more ways to express the intricate, important idea of "honor" than we have in English.

That afternoon, I spoke with a VITO on the phone. As our conversation drew to a close, I said, "VITO, it was a real honor to speak with you today." And an amazing thing happened. VITO said, "That's an interesting word. I've never heard a salesperson use that word before—or anyone in this company, for that matter. Why do you feel it was an honor to talk to me?"

"VITO," I said, "you're the one person who truly understands where your company has to go, and the one person with the vision to guide it to that place. You've given me an opportunity to look at things in your world. Now I feel very close to your organization; I feel that I really understand how I can help you in what you're trying to do. And to me, it's an honor to be in that position."

If you can reach that point of understanding, you will be able to say—with complete honesty—exactly what I said that afternoon to that VITO. You'll be able to say it not only to your business contacts, but to others in your life, and you will be able to extend *and* rely on the kind of loyalty that really makes life meaningful. You'll be able to show that you truly honor your relationships. And you'll have made my work as a teacher worthwhile.

All the success!

TONY PARINELLO

APPENDIX A:
YOUR PROSPECTING RATIO

In this part of the book, we'll look at the formulas you will need to use to forecast your own sales targets in your daily sales work. Don't leave this work to your sales manager; take control of your own career and monitor your own ratios.

Definitions

A *suspect* is a company representative or decision maker in your product or service market within the territory you've been assigned.

A *prospect* is a suspect you've contacted who has needs that are similar to those you have met successfully in other accounts.

A *hot lead* is a prospect who will give you an equal shot at winning the business, someone you could win within the context of your normal sales cycle. Typically, you have met with this person, looked at the mutual opportunities, and given at least an overview of your products, services, and solutions.

Step One: Targets

Monitor your own sales work for one month (or whatever period is appropriate in your industry) and answer these questions:

If you contacted 100 suspects (via telephone calls, mailings, in-person meetings, or a combination of these), how many prospects would result? Write your answer here: (A)_____

How many of the prospects you identified in (A) would turn into hot leads? Write your answer here: (B)_____

How many of the hot leads you identified in (B) would you turn into actual sales? Write your answer here: (C)_____

[This page intentionally blank.]

Step Two: Ratio

Divide the number on line C by 100. The result is your ratio. Write your answer here: (R)_____

Step Three: Goals

Fill in the blanks.

What is your yearly quota or sales goal, in dollars?
(I) _____

What are your projected sales totals, in dollars, from current customers?
(II) _____

Subtract Item II from Item I to yield the amount of new sales dollars needed this year.

(III) _____

Enter the dollar amount of your average sale.
(IV) _____

Divide Item III by Item IV to yield the number of new sales needed this year.
(V) _____

Step Four: Task

Divide the number in item V by your ratio (line R in Step Two). Write your answer here. _____

This is the number of new suspects you will need to contact in the coming year to reach your yearly target. Now divide that number by 52, and you'll know how many suspects you must contact each week to make your quota.

Note: Aim high! I always shoot for 125% of quota if I want to hit 110%!

APPENDIX B:
THE TEMPLATE OF IDEAL PROSPECTS (TIP) AND THE BENEFIT MATRIX

A "Tip" You Can Count On!

When completed, this exercise will provide you with vital information that will assist you in qualifying new prospects before and during the first sales call. Your Template of Ideal Prospects (TIP) will help you compare your best customers to new prospects—and show you where your best opportunities lie.

To identify your very best existing customer(s), find answers to the key questions in the following categories and record them in the chart provided on page 227.

Company data. In the distribution industry, for example, you might list: number of parts in inventory; seasonal needs; purchasing habits on critical components; shipping unit size; order origin and entry procedures (processed from catalog? counter? telephone?); fleet owned or leased; number of employees; annual revenue; number of salespeople; etc.

Relevant sales parameter data. Determine: specific problems solved through use of your product or service; third-party "value-added" products or services necessary to secure the sale; price sensitivity among key decision makers; your price position among competitors; titles of key contacts.

Tangible and intangible benefits. Highlight the specific, quantifiable benefits this customer is realizing as a result of using your solution and having a business relationship with your company.

That's What Your Happy Customer Looks Like

There will be some exceptions, but generally, prospects with profiles that show extreme differences from those of your best customer(s)

225

should be avoided or placed on the far back burner. While it is not necessary for you to do exhaustive research in preparation for a call on a new prospect, you may do so if you wish. It is essential, though, to have a strong sense of the profile of your *current* satisfied customers, and to be ready to "fill in the blanks" of your templates as you learn more about new opportunities.

Industry _____

1.

Profile: Best Customer: _____	Profile: This Prospect: _____	Match?

2.

Notes: _____

3.

Benefits: _____

Appendix C:
Talk Back!

I want to hear about what you think of the *Selling to VITO* program! If you have comments, questions, or suggestions on how the system can be improved, please take a moment to write them below and send them to the address that appears at the bottom of this page. I will personally answer all this correspondence.

Thanks!

_____

_____

_____

_____

_____

_____

_____

_____

_____

_____

_____

_____

_____

_____

_____

Send to: Anthony Parinello, *Selling to VITO*, c/o Bob Adams, Inc., 260 Center Street, Holbrook, Massachusetts 02343. All letters become the property of Parinello Incorporated.

INDEX

YOUR FASTEST WAY TO SUCCESS

The complete *"Selling to VITO"* product line will teach you how to: convert your product knowledge into *VITO*'s knowledge, speak *VITO*'s language, write the one piece of correspondence that gets up to a 40% in-person appointment ratio with *VITO*, create the best eight second telephone opening statements to get *VITO*'s attention, get by receptionist gatekeepers and win the respect of *VITO*'s personal assistant, leave messages that get return calls and how to leave the ultimate voice mail message for *VITO* that puts the spotlight on you! You'll also learn all the how-to's of answering every single initial objection you may get from *VITO* and ask the three most important questions during your first sales call.

I could go on and on about all the tactics and skill building information you'll be able to master, but right now it's your turn to take the next step into *VITO*'s office!

CALL 1-800-777-VITO TO ORDER YOUR PERSONAL SUCCESS KIT.

Audio Album

Six audio cassettes, a workbook, and Personal Action Guide on diskette. Listen, learn, and master all the tactics you need to get on *VITO*'s calendar right from your car, at home, or at work! Your Master Key to the Executive Suite.

Appointment Getting Cards for VITO

Perfect for every business occasion, including prospecting, follow-up or getting *VITO* to return your calls. Includes software to enable personalized captions with *VITO*'s name in it! There's not a gatekeeper in the world that will stop this card from going on the top of *VITO*'s in-basket! A perfect way to set yourself above and beyond your competition.

Additional Copies of *Selling to VITO* Paperback

230 pages of the best selling tactics and skills you'll need to become a total success in getting more appointments at the top! Easy and entertaining to read.

Proven *VITO* Letters & Opening Statements

Examples from the best *VITO* letters in the world! Letters that have earned millions of dollars in sales commissions! Cut and paste from plenty of samples. This disk also includes the best opening statements that Tony has ever created and is guaranteed to make the best first telephone impression ever!

Voice Mail Messages to *VITO*

Audio cassette with workbook on diskette. Learn the most critical ingredients and the best words and phrases to use to get a call back from *VITO*. Includes scripts with proven results!

***Selling to VITO* InstaView**

A unique computer program combining a screen saver with the electronic version of *Selling to VITO*. The entire book is on disk—with powerful search, key words, navigation features and much more! Users need only a personal computer (PC) with Microsoft Windows.

Here's my unique guarantee:

Order any of my *Selling to VITO* products and receive my prove it to yourself guarantee. Listen, learn and experience my products for 30 days. If you are not absolutely, overwhelmingly and totally convinced that my methods, tactics and ideas will get you appointments at the top where sales cycles are shorter and opportunities are greater, you can send your products back and get a FULL refund. It's that simple.

"Tony's been in the field and his tactics come from practical experience, not from a textbook."

— Jack Slotow, Oakbrook, IL

"After 14 years in sales to Fortune 500 companies with reputations of having the best training programs, I was amazed at the number of powerful, creative new ideas I learned from Tony and his products to excel in my sales career."

— Alice Prais, Highwood, IL

About the Author

Anthony Parinello is one of the most innovative sales trainers in America today. His passion is his sales and public speaking career. When he's not on the speaking platform, you can find Tony with his wife Nancy trekking in the Himalayas, scuba diving in Palau, on a photographic safari in Africa, or in any number of other exotic locales. Mr. and Mrs. Parinello live in California.